The Bionic People Are Here

DR. ARTHUR S. FREESE

The Bionic People Are Here

ILLUSTRATED WITH PHOTOGRAPHS

McGRAW-HILL BOOK COMPANY

New York • St. Louis • San Francisco • Auckland •
Bogotá • Düsseldorf • Johannesburg • London • Madrid •
Mexico • Montreal • New Delhi • Panama • Paris •
São Paulo • Singapore • Sydney • Tokyo • Toronto

Library of Congress Cataloging in Publication Data

Freese, Arthur S.
  The bionic people are here.
  Bibliography: p.
  Includes index.
  SUMMARY: Surveys the history of implants and transplants and
discusses in detail what is being done, how, and where in the
human body, the problems encountered and implications for the
future.
  1. Transplantation of organs, tissues, etc.—Juvenile
literature. 2. Prosthesis—Juvenile literature.
[1. Transplantation of organs, tissues, etc. 2. Prosthesis] I. Title.
RD120.7.F73   617'.95   78-8253
ISBN 0-07-022133-2

123456789 BPBP 7832109

Contents

CONTENTS

Acknowledgments

It is impossible to name everyone who has helped with this book, but I would like particularly to express my thanks and appreciation to these medical scientists who have so generously given of their time and expertise:

Dr. Willem J. Kolff, Director of the Institute for Biomedical Engineering, University of Utah, whose invention of the artificial kidney has already saved tens of thousands of lives and whose continuing research into artificial organs has truly opened and inspired the era of the bionic people.

Dr. Robert W. Mann, Professor of Biomedical Engineering, Massachusetts Institute of Technology, and leading developer of artificial limbs.

Dr. Clement B. Sledge, Surgeon-in-Chief, Robert B. Brigham Hospital, Boston, Massachusetts, a pioneer in the treatment of arthritis and the development and insertion of total artificial arm and leg joints.

Thanks must also be expressed to the following institutions and their information specialists who have helped:

Battelle Memorial Institute of Columbus, Ohio
Duke University Medical Center

ACKNOWLEDGMENTS

National Bureau of Standards
The Pennsylvania State University
Stanford University Medical Center
University of Michigan Medical Center
And thanks here to those others who are too numerous to
name but who also helped . . .

A.S.F.

The Bionic People
Are Here

PART I

The Myth and the Reality: Past, Present, and Future

You can see them on your TV screen: the Bionic Woman, the Six Million Dollar Man—and now there's Max the Bionic Dog as well! These super-beings are supposedly rebuilt from the wreckage of the ordinary human or animal who has met with an almost impossible-to-imagine destruction of bones, muscles, and organs. Their crushed and smashed skeletons and every organ except the brain have been rebuilt with artificial parts.

This fictional bionic result is presented as a bigger, better, stronger, and faster version of the original mortal creature. It's a one-of-a-kind creation, seemingly unique to the Space Age with its amazing new medicine, surgery, and bioengineering. But this is not actually true! Not just one man and one woman but millions of everyday Americans actually become bionic people every year, and the means for such creations are being increased or improved all the time.

The word "bionics" is actually defined differently in various dictionaries and encyclopedias. Usually, it is considered either a science or a branch of science which,

1

in general, combines the knowledge of engineering and artificial systems with the characteristics of biological and living organisms to produce devices or systems with the advantages of both. The *Encyclopaedia Britannica* credits the coining of the term to U.S. Air Force Major Jack E. Steele of the Aerospace Division, who applied it to the construction of such combined systems in 1958. So to be bionic, a person really needs only some of these combinations. He need not be all-artificial as the current crop of TV characters imply.

The production of a bionic person has been dreamed of since the beginning of human history, when earliest man or pre-man emerged several million years ago. Moreover, natural transplants and implanted artificial organs were inserted into people some six thousand years ago—and very likely even earlier.

Mythology has always played a part in human societies. In July 1914, a French professor and his three young sons were vacationing in the foothills of the Pyrenees in Southern France when they stumbled upon a cave now named Les Trois Frères. Lowered by rope into the cave, one of the youngsters returned to tell of hundreds of paintings on the walls. One of these has since been proven to be a 20,000-year-old rendering of a bionic person—a Stone Age medicine man with the head, face, hump, tail, and front hooves of a bison, but with his own human feet.

For more than six thousand years Greek mythology prominently featured transplants from animal to man and animal to animal. The Chimera, depicted so often in Greek art, was a fire-breathing female monster with the head and front part of a lion, the middle of a goat, and the rear and tail of a dragon. The earliest Egyptian papyruses tell of the caste of tile-makers whose responsibility was the transplanting of skin grafts.

2

And some three thousand years ago, the Hindu surgeon Susruta was justly famous throughout the ancient world for transplanting skin to repair ears and noses. (In those days, noses were often cut off as a punishment for adultery.) Susruta would slice off a flap of skin from the cheek and carefully position it so as to rebuild the nose. Temporarily holding the flap in position with bandages and with sutures (stitches) of cotton, hair, animal sinews, hemp, or even leather, the Hindu surgeon maintained the blood supply by leaving this skin attached by its base to the cheek until it had grown into place on the nose and had established a new blood supply there. Only then did he sever the original connections to the cheek. His amazingly modern technique, now known as the "sliding flap," is still used today.

This interest in bionic people has reappeared in each succeeding era. It's part of many early Christian legends, and the folktales of the Middle Ages often describe the transplantation of noses and even whole limbs from one person to another. In fact, a fifteenth-century Italian painting depicts the replacement of a cancerous leg with a healthy one from a corpse—a sort of preview of Frankenstein's monster and our current use of cadaver parts for transplantation. A semblance of reality was even given to such visionary dreams by Lazzaro Spallanzani, greatest of the eighteenth-century physiologists, those scientists concerned with the functioning of the living organism. In 1768 Spallanzani published the results of his varied experiments in transplantation and regeneration. In one of these experiments he successfully transplanted the head of one snail onto the body of another.

But it wasn't until the early nineteenth century that the modern world of transplants (natural organs and tissues) and implants (artificial substitutes) had its real beginning. One could truly say that the 1800s saw the birth of

3

today's bionic people. For early in the last century, ophthalmologists (eye specialists and surgeons) noted that injuries or diseases sometimes caused the cornea to turn opaque. The victim would lose his vision.

The normal healthy cornea is a dime-sized structure, tough but perfectly transparent, which covers the front of the eyeball. It protects your eyeball and sharpens your vision by helping to focus light rays. Contemplating the problem, the ophthalmologists were seized by the exciting concept of a clear replacement for such opaque corneas. These specialists proceeded to experiment with anything that was transparent—glass, celluloid, even the corneas of lower animals—in search of a substitute for the clouded natural cornea.

Out of this ferment came the first successful corneal transplant. This initial operation was performed by a prisoner of the Arabs in 1835, a British Army surgeon, Dr. S. L. Bigger. After being captured by Bedouins, he acquired a pet, an antelope that had only one eye. To make matters worse, the cornea of that one eye was so badly scarred that its vision had been lost, too. Evidently familiar with the ophthalmologic activity of his day, Bigger removed the cornea from a recently killed antelope and transplanted it onto the eye of his own pet. The whole upper half of this corneal transplant retained its transparency, and the vision of his pet was restored. It was an amazing achievement for that time.

During the nineteenth century there were other bright spots in the growing field of bionics. In 1823 a plastic surgeon—Dr. Christian Heinrich Bunger—was able to report the first successful modern skin transplant, a reconstruction of a woman's nose with skin from her thigh. Bunger's success inspired further attempts at corneal transplants from animals to humans. But there were

4

surgical infections and the corneal grafts became clouded, so surgeons went back to artificial substitutes with at least some success.

An Austrian ophthalmologist, a Dr. Heusser, tried implanting a piece of glass in a girl's eye with temporary success. This same result was achieved by Germany's Dr. Arthur Van Hippel when he tried a removable gold-rimmed glass lens. Actually, it was not until 1905 that Dr. Eduard Zirm, from what is now Czechoslovakia, finally carried out the first successful human-to-human corneal transplant.

But the path to the bionic people has been a rocky one, with problems plaguing those who attempted to transplant natural organs and tissues from one person to another, or from animal to person. Similarly, those who have striven for the implantation of artificial replacements and devices have also encountered great difficulties. However, the nineteenth century clarified some of the problems and made it possible to understand why others arose.

In 1865 Scottish surgeon Joseph Lister opened the door to the brilliant successful surgery of modern times by introducing antiseptic techniques. These eliminated the threat of infection, which had always made surgery and hospitals a nightmare of gangrene and death. Surgeons could now begin to dream of and perform operations they had never before dared attempt, and to succeed with procedures that had previously shown unbelievably high mortality rates. Gone for the first time was the spectre of fatal infections that had menaced anyone who suffered a compound fracture of the arm or leg. (In these fractures, the bone breaks through the skin.)

This new control of infection together with the 1896 discovery of X rays served to unveil the existence of

5

another problem—the reaction of the body to such foreign materials as the metal sutures, wires, and screws used in the treatment of bone fractures. The vast surgical and medical revolution wrought by the transplantation of natural organs and tissues, and the implantation of a wide variety of artificial parts from head to toe, has really come about only since the late 1930s and World War II. It required the introduction of new materials that the body could tolerate, the understanding of the body's reaction to other people's organs and tissues, and the extensive development of artificial joints.

MENDING WITH METALS

The use of metals in the human body in a variety of forms and for a wide range of purposes has evidently only been limited by their availability. Mankind has known gold, silver, and copper—even iron found in fallen meteorites—for more than six thousand years simply because these materials existed in pure form on the earth's surface during prehistoric times. Gold was most likely the first known, for nuggets were often found in the early riverbeds. Since gold tended to keep both its luster and its color, it must have attracted early man's attention. In fact, some six thousand years ago, the Phoenicians were already able to produce gold wire from pure gold because pure gold is soft and can be easily manipulated. They even used it to splint loose teeth and replace missing ones.

About this time, too, the ancient Egyptian physicians used silver plates to close skull wounds. The ancient Chinese are supposed to have inserted gold and silver acupuncture needles into ailing people. And three thousand years ago, the Etruscans were soldering gold bands, not unlike today's orthodontic braces, and then riveting animal or human teeth to these to replace missing human teeth. Five hundred years later Hippocrates, the "father of medicine," used gold wires for sutures, and some sixteenth- and seventeenth-century medical experts were still advising sutures of gold, iron, and bronze wires made flexible by heat. Even brass wires were used for holding broken bones together to help them heal.

In 1565 a gold plate was used to close a cleft palate, and during the eighteenth century iron wires were implanted to hold fractured bones together. But in the nineteenth century there came a breakthrough in this area. Screws, pins, and metal wires were introduced to hold together both the broken bones and their joints, so that the bones could still be used for walking while healing was taking place. Even more like the bionic man's parts were the metal plates or bars screwed to the fractured bone. These bridged the break and held the parts together, supporting as well as strengthening the fracture. Silver sutures were introduced by Dr. J. Marion Sims, the famous American surgeon and gynecologist, just before our Civil War.

This use of metal implants brought forth new problems, however. At first the doctors blamed the metal itself for the infections that resulted. But the new antiseptic surgery clarified the picture, and the X ray made it possible to see just what was happening to both the metal implants and the bones involved. Now that the surgeons were themselves no longer introducing infections, they could distinguish between what was tissue reaction to the metal and what was infection introduced by the pre-sterile operating techniques.

But now let us look more closely at the problems that have complicated the advent of the bionic people.

HOW YOUR OWN BODY WORKS

The human body is a complex mixture of electrical, chemical, and mechanical processes, any of which can and often does go awry. In the past little could be done when some part such as a kidney, heart, or joint broke down. But now it's a whole different ball game! Doctors, surgeons, and engineers are working together to understand your body and how it works so that they can perform medical miracles should things go haywire. Let us look at some of their findings.

Your mind and nerves transmit messages and orders electrically and chemically. These pass to and from your brain and spinal cord along nerves. Some of these nerves extend all the way from your toes right up to your head. Other nerves, however, travel no farther than the distance from your eyes to the back part of your brain, the visual center.

Your blood is a combination of fluid, red and white blood cells, and platelets, each with its own tasks. In this fluid are carried oxygen, carbon dioxide, acids, salt, and a host of other powerful chemicals. Red cells carry oxygen, white cells destroy foreign invaders such as bacteria or viruses, and platelets promote clotting so that a cut blood vessel or skin wound doesn't keep on bleeding. The bloodstream picks up the waste materials produced when your muscles and other tissues do their jobs. These wastes are carried to the kidneys, which act as a blood-cleansing system, filtering the blood and then eliminating the waste products and the toxic (poisonous) materials that accumulate in the bloodstream.

Your joints make it possible for you to move flexibly, to bend at right angles, to turn and pivot, to walk or run, and to throw a football or swing a baseball bat. And with all these actions or processes, the miracle is that you need give your body no thought. It does its job automatically, with no conscious direction or even awareness on your own part: your heart speeds up, you breathe faster, the right muscles contract at the appropriate time.

Brain, bones, kidneys, and joints—all are crucial to our functioning. But the new wonder is that when something goes terribly wrong with these vital parts of our bodies, doctors can replace them with natural or artificial substitutes. In short, this is the age of the bionic people!

WHY TRANSPLANTS AND ARTIFICIAL PARTS CAUSE PROBLEMS

The biological, medical, and physical sciences had to be developed to a very sophisticated stage before the body's reaction to transplants and artificial parts could even be understood. For these reactions to either natural or artificial parts are extremely complex and reflect the body's basic nature. Some are the result of the body's own chemistry, and some arise from the very mechanisms that nature herself put there to protect us from infection by such disease-producing organisms as bacteria or viruses, or such intruding foreign materials as splinters of wood or metal.

During the Civil War, for the first time, it became generally recognized that when skin was transplanted from one person to another the donor tissue would die, be rejected by the recipient. To understand this phenomenon of rejection—whether of transplanted heart, kidney, skin, or any other organ—we must first look at the body's immune system. This is the way the body protects itself, distinguishes "self" from "not-self." Vital as this immune system is to the control of infection, it can destroy

9

transplants—and when it goes haywire, it can lead to serious trouble.

If our immune system failed to tell self from not-self, our protective mechanisms—both chemical and cellular—would turn on us and destroy our very own tissues. In fact, there are diseases that today are suspected of being the result of just such a confusion. One theory about rheumatoid arthritis, for example, is that the body loses the ability to recognize its joint tissues as part of itself and so attacks them, destroying the joints.

People have always recognized that something was wrong when some body spot, say on their hand or foot, became red, hot, tender, and swollen. And two thousand years ago Aulus Cornelius Celsus—the greatest Roman medical writer—described these four changes as the cardinal signs of inflammation. This process is triggered to varying degrees by any insult to living tissues: a cut or burn; an infection; or some irritant, such as a splinter in the skin. Our bodies are programmed by nature to eliminate these problems. Inflammation is a protective mechanism meant to bring the whole immunological power of the body to bear on the offending substance and destroy it, to protect the integrity and health of the person.

While repairing your bicycle, you might cut your finger or get a metal splinter in it. The finger then gets red and sore, perhaps swells. This all shows that the protective inflammatory reaction is working for you. An increased blood flow to the area causes the redness and the heat, as it brings white blood cells (the lymphocytes in particular), whose task it is to attack and destroy the offending objects. This attack-destroy mission is accomplished either by the release of powerful chemicals or by the cells swallowing the substance (which may be any foreign body or protein—bacteria, dead bodily tissue resulting from a burn, or a wood or metal splinter). Fluid blood (plasma) seeps out of the blood vessels, causing swelling and bringing other chemicals, antibodies, as well as more white cells to bear on the offender.

When the problem is resolved, the whole process reverses itself and the inflammation subsides. It's all part of the immune system, the method nature has evolved over the last half billion years for our protection. It first began among the earliest bony fishes and is limited to the vertebrates, those animals with spinal or vertebral columns.

The very word "immunity" was first applied to a fifteenth-century practice in which men who had survived the Black Death were exempted from military service and were instead drafted as nurses for the plague victims. And modern immunology began in the eighteenth century, when Edward Jenner, an English physician, noticed that dairymaids who contracted cowpox from milking an animal with the disease didn't get smallpox. All the dairymaids suffered was a small pustule, a sore full of pus.

Taking the pus from a cowpox sore, Jenner put it under the skin of a healthy 8-year-old boy. The boy developed a small sore and then a scab. The scab fell off, leaving a small scar. Six weeks later Jenner exposed the boy to smallpox—and he proved immune! With the widespread routine use of this vaccination, smallpox has been virtually eliminated from the face of the earth. When it is gone from a small spot in East Africa, it will be the first disease that man has wiped off the entire earth. And it couldn't have happened without our immune system.

This system is dependent on proteins called antigens and body chemicals called antibodies. These work much

11

like a lock and key, opposite parts of the same system. The antigen is the protein of the invader—of the bacteria or virus—which can enter the body by inhalation or injection or through a cut. The antigen may even be the protein of an organ, such as a kidney or heart implanted in an operation. Any substance (such as a virus with its protein coat) that can set off an immune reaction can act as an antigen. However, these do vary in their antigenicity, their ability to produce an immune response, with their degree of "foreignness." Thus, there is less antigenicity in transplanted tissues from a brother or sister than from a stranger, and none at all in those from identical twins who are formed from the same egg and sperm and so have identical genes and genetic characteristics. (Doctors have found that a piece of skin transplanted from one identical twin to the other produces no immune reaction but grows there as if it were the recipient's own.) The antibodies are the defenders, with certain white blood cells (the lymphocytes) acting as sort of roving, patrolling guardians.

When an invading foreign protein—bacterium or virus, blood transfusion, transplant—enters the body, the complex immune system checks it out. Once the material has been identified as foreign, this complex system quickly mobilizes its forces to attack. There is an inflammatory reaction, and lymphocytes gather. Some of these blood cells, the B cells, manufacture the antibodies to coat the invader and destroy it; another type, the T cells, go after the foreign matter to digest, break down, and destroy it.

The immune system has no way of knowing that a transplant has been put there to help and not harm the body. So the system reacts to transplants as it does to any foreign protein. It attacks, rejects, the transplant, and that is the chief reason why transplants fail. However, medical scientists have learned to circumvent this problem in one of two ways. If an identical twin can be the donor and provide the needed organ, there is no rejection because the antigens of donor and recipient are identical. Otherwise, doctors match antigens to the best of the current knowledge about such matching: termed tissue typing, this is actually done by testing the similarity and compatibility of a whole range of complex proteins and antigens in the blood and choosing the closest match.

Doctors then administer so-called immunosuppressive drugs, which reduce the ability of the donor's body to mount an effective immune response. This makes it possible for even foreign tissues or organs to be tolerated without rejection. Unfortunately, this also tends to leave the person susceptible to infections. It takes what amounts to some complex medical tightrope-walking to strike a healthy balance: doctors must provide enough immunosuppression to protect the transplant but not so much as to totally deprive the recipient of all protection from infection.

Some tissues are safer than others from immune response. Corneal transplants from cadavers can be used without tissue typing or immunosuppressive drugs because of this tissue's unique characteristics. The cornea normally receives no blood supply but is fed by the diffusion of nutrients from neighboring structures and tissue fluids. Since it is the blood that produces the immune reaction, transplanted corneas are protected from this problem and not rejected as are the heart, lungs, or other organs or tissues being transplanted.

Quite different from the problems of transplantation, however, are those presented by artificial implants. As Dr. Patrick G. Laing, a University of Pittsburgh professor of orthopedic surgery, sums it up: "It is not enough that we just examine the physical properties and the behavior of an implant; we must also realize it is being placed in a human being and this human being is a complicated chemical factory in which we have yet to assess the effects of released metal ions or enzymes or breakdown products. . . . " These varied implants range today from metal and plastic joints to heart valves and electrodes.

Doctors must not only consider the effects of these foreign materials on the body but must also understand the body's effect on these implants. It's a little hard for people to realize that the body's inner environment—the tissues with their fluids and the blood itself—is an intensely hostile and corrosive one, whose harsh threat makes a salt spray, the usual industrial corrosion test for metals, seem gentle and benign by comparison. For the body's salinity is even greater than that of sea water, but with oxygen, chlorine, and a host of other powerful chemicals and organic acids all added. Not surprisingly, there are few materials that can serve in such an atmosphere without corroding. For example, one must not mix different metals. If a bar or plate of titanium is held by a screw of any other metal, the metals will react where they touch each other and corrode. This corrosion will cause tissue inflammation and/or metal breakage.

Then, too, the body reacts to the very materials used or to their corrosion by-products. Such tissue reactions may trigger inflammation with pain or pus formation. There may even be an actual resorption of the bone to loosen the implant. Initially screwed into the hard bone and held there, the screws may loosen as the bone softens about them, in which case the implant can actually be dislodged.

Metals and plates must not only be inert (causing no reaction on the part of the tissues), but the material must

also be surprisingly strong for ordinary human use—
without any extraordinary demands such as those of the
bionic TV characters, who can bend metal bars with
bare hands or shatter a wall with one blow. Your hip
joint, for example, must support four to seven times your
entire body weight whenever you walk. To be strong
enough for wide use in bone repairs or replacements, a
material must be able to carry a load of 100,000 pounds
per square inch (p.s.i.) without deforming or giving. The
hard outer layer of mature human bone is able to take a
pressure of about 20,000 p.s.i. In addition, the material
should show no corrosion and produce neither inflammatory nor other tissue or bodily reactions even after
being in position for many years. This is particularly
important today when many people in their teens and
others even younger are having implants—bone plates and
screws for fractured bones, joints for arthritic problems,
corrective measures for a variety of birth defects or
disease conditions.

The plastic materials used must not only be inert and
nontoxic, but must be able to take stress, friction, and
heat, for such materials often form part of joints or valves
in the heart where considerable and almost constant
friction as well as pressure is applied to them. And,
finally, there is methylmethacrylate, the plastic or polymer cement used to hold joints and bones in place: mixed
as a liquid and a powder and packed into the bones
in a semi-soft or moist state, the liquid can be ab-
sorbed. Therefore, the material must be inert so that it
doesn't provoke a reaction elsewhere in the body should
the blood carry some of it throughout the circulatory
system.

There is a whole range of materials used in heart valves
and for repairing or replacing sections of arteries and

blood vessels. As Dr. Leslie Smith of the National Bureau of Standards (NBS) Polymer Stability and Reactivity Section explains: "Cardiovascular (heart and blood vessel) implants pose different problems than do orthopedic (bone) implants. . . . the major concern is the compatibility of the implant with blood. All materials used to date have tended to damage red blood cells and other elements of the blood, promote clotting, or denature blood and plasma proteins."

In addition, the material must be tough and flexible, and remain this way through many decades of hard wear. The problem with our current materials which do tend to produce clots on their surface is a vital one—for such clots invariably present the danger that they will break off and go sailing through the arteries until they finally reach one that is too small to pass through. When this happens the blood flow is dammed up and some area of the body is cheated of its blood (and so its oxygen and food) supply. Sooner or later, depending on whether the organ tissues involved have other blood supplies and whether the artery supplies a larger or vital area, the organ will die. Should this occur in such a vital organ as the lung, brain, or heart, the victim may become acutely ill, be paralyzed, or may even die.

The search for perfect materials goes on—a search for strong, noncorroding, nontoxic, and inert metals and plastics, for others that will not affect the blood and its cells. According to the NBS: "When it comes to the human body and the myriad materials that could possibly be used, there are no easy answers. But scientists, surgeons, and other specialists are searching deeply into the problems presented by both in the hope of making the tricky replacement of worn-out body parts safer and more reliable."

BIONICS TODAY: THE STATE OF THE ART

As we've seen, in the broad sense, these bionic people have actually been around for a long time. However, as a science applying Space Age technology and engineering to the human being, bionics is very new. Certainly, there is virtually no area of the body at least some of whose problems are not being successfully attacked by bionics —by Space Age medicine, surgery, and bioengineering. Skull plates are old stuff, true, but these were not made of the exotic metals now being used (tantalum) or the new plastics (polyethylene). Shunts (tiny tubes) are being implanted in the brain to relieve a variety of ailments. They even restored one of our national heroes to his brilliant role in our space program, from which he'd been forced to retire because of an ear impairment. The blind are being made to see and the deaf to hear. And all of this is being accomplished by daring medical innovators and pioneers who implant electrodes in the skull and even in the very brain tissue itself.

Today, artificial elements of the intestinal tract are run outside the body so that people can eat again; artificial teeth implanted in the jaws take root like the missing ones; artificial hearts pump away, keeping living creatures alive for a half year and more; and new valves are installed in hearts. Other electronic devices called pacemakers make the heart beat properly and have benefitted countless people, from former Supreme Court Justice William O. Douglas and actor Henry Fonda to a 26-hour-old premature infant. Virtually every arm and leg joint can be replaced by artificial substitute. Increasingly, the use of these devices and transplants is being extended to people of all ages.

Young people—injured in our increasingly active

17

society—are getting a variety of mechanical aids and artificial limbs and parts inside and outside the body. Even those who have lost limbs can get new ones that they can use almost as well as they once used their very own. Powerful magnets helped rebuild the destroyed face of a Boston teenager. And the artificial kidney is saving the lives of uncounted young people whose natural organ has failed them. Soon it may even be possible to simply wear one of these devices during one's ordinary daily activities or while traveling instead of spending long hours sitting or lying immobilized while the job of cleansing the blood of impurities is carried out by a large and unwieldy machine.

Young people, too, are coming in for their share of transplants. Increasingly, youngsters are being given natural new kidneys to replace their own destroyed ones, so they need no longer suffer with the artificial ones. In fact, kidney transplants are so common that they are considered routine operations today. There are artificial hearts and heart devices, an artificial pancreas—and even an artificial gut in use today!

The number of those benefitting from these medical marvels is mind-boggling. Figures from the NBS reveal that in the United States alone more than a million individual artificial implants are placed in people every year. These devices range from the total artificial joints all the way down to heart valves and bone plates, screws, nails, and pins. In fact, one of today's problems has arisen from the very degree of the success obtained, for doctors are now more confident and willing to use these on teenagers and younger people. The result is that where such devices were once considered satisfactory if they stood up adequately for a decade or two, now they must be able to last for thirty or forty years. Unfortunately, the ideal materials for these long-lasting implants are yet to be found.

The most commonly used materials today, according to the NBS, are the special surgical stainless steels. Most stainless steel, however, cannot stand up to the rigors of the body's inner environment. Other effective materials include the cobalt-chromium alloys and the titanium alloys. These are used to make a variety of appliances, such as heart valves; plates to bridge and hold together fractured sections of bones until healing is completed, or to strengthen diseased bones; metal nails and pins to accomplish these same purposes in the long bones of the arms and legs; and, finally, screws to hold some of these appliances in position. In many cases, various plastics such as methylmethacrylate polymers, polyethylene, or Teflon are used in heart valves or body joints, or as cements.

Meanwhile, bionic men and women are being created in vast numbers today and with surprising success. The medical and engineering sciences have combined to circumvent and outwit nature's immune system and inflammatory processes, to slip into the human body a wide range of materials and devices, as well as other people's organs and tissues. Kidneys are being replaced both with artificial devices and with natural organs. And in Europe, ceramic replacements are being tried more widely than here in the United States—and now come bones of glass!

A glass-ceramic material called bioglass has moved from the animal experimentation stage to actual use in human beings. This material contains some of the very elements found in natural bone: calcium and phosphorus in particular. When a bioglass implant contacts natural bone, the two fuse together much as our own bones knit after a fracture, thus eliminating the need for the usual screws and other attaching devices or materials. Experts think bioglass might well be the way to save badly shattered or diseased arms and legs from amputation.

There are also tissue glues, which someday may even eliminate the need for many of the surgeon's needles and threads. Amazing adhesives, the so-called cyanoacrylates are so powerful that when they are attached to a grand piano or to a car, those heavy objects can be lifted by the strength of the bond alone.

So there *are* bionic people today. But these are scientific realities, people with human limitations and capacities, bionic beings but not super-beings. They are being created virtually every hour in hospital operating rooms all over the world.

Madeleine Jacobs, an NBS expert, sums up the extent of such surgical implants this way: "Thousands of people are leading active lives today thanks to the progress made by the medical and surgical professions in simulating and replacing defective body parts with man-made devices. In the United States alone, more than one million individual orthopedic implants are surgically inserted each year, ranging from metal nails and screws to plates, pins, and prostheses (artificial replacements of body parts). At least forty-five thousand artificial heart valves and a hundred thousand artificial arteries have been implanted since they were first developed."

But, she continues: "Despite these successes, the reliability and durability of many synthetic materials implanted in the human body are matters of increasing concern. One reason is the trend toward implantation in younger and more active patients. Until recently, implants generally were inserted only in elderly patients. . . ."

THE ROAD AHEAD: THE NEW SURGICAL ERA OF REPLACEMENT THERAPY

Dr. William H. Dobelle, Director of the Division of Artificial Organs, Department of Surgery, at New York's Columbia-Presbyterian Medical Center, sees a whole new world opening up before us. When he talks, the listener can see the hope for bionic people as a very real scientific possibility! Asked where we were realistically headed in this new world of artificial organs, this national expert answered without hesitation. "I have the feeling that nothing is impossible—how long it may take, how complicated it may be, and whether it will be desirable depends on the individual project. But I don't think there are any intrinsic limitations—with the exception of the nervous system. Heart, lung, kidney, liver, pancreas replacements, for example, are fairly straightforward—but the nervous system is quite another thing, and if there's any place you're going to run into fundamental limitations it's going to be here."

Actually, Dr. Dobelle sees transplantation and the use of artificial organs going hand-in-hand. In fact, it is the success of the artificial kidney that has really made kidney transplantation so successful today. As the doctor explains: "Transplantation and artificial organs are complementary—certainly not competitive." A realist as well as a pioneer in this exciting new medical and surgical world, Dr. Dobelle talked frankly about the future: "A severed spinal cord in a quadriplegic or paraplegic is much more . . . complicated than say a total artificial heart. Obviously too, replacing the spinal cord is easier than thinking of trying to replace a portion of the brain damaged by stroke, for example. But here you're getting yourself into additional levels of complexity, so

21

far in excess of anything we're attacking now that one has to be realistic about it."

Summing this all up, he said: "You're seeing a burgeoning and developing technology, and looking ahead I think one is always very foolish to say 'Well, you can do everything but you can't do x'—because twenty-five years ago if you . . . proposed to someone that people would be seriously considering artificial vision for the blind, I'm not sure that you would have been taken very seriously. However, I'm most reluctant to state that something is impossible—but I also hesitate to say when it will be realized."

Finally, Dr. Dobelle spoke of his vision of what the future is likely to be: "You're looking ahead to the era of replacement therapy—where you replace the whole organ. In a way it's almost the same as when your TV goes bad and they don't try to fix the individual transistor but pull out the whole board and replace it—or when your car's transmission needs fixing: in the old days they would change the seals or whatever but the rest would only break down again later, where today they yank the whole thing and replace it. I think that's what you're going to start seeing in the future—when somebody's got a diseased heart nobody is going to bother changing the diseased heart valve or bypassing the coronary arteries and the rest. If the heart is that diseased, you will just take it out and replace it with a new system! That's the direction we will go."

The father of artificial organs is the great international figure Dr. Willem J. Kolff, who invented the artificial kidney in Holland during World War II. Now at the University of Utah, he sums up the future for transplants and artificial devices: "In transplants there is a limitation of supply, but for artificial organs there is not—there is only a limitation of engineering, and the development will probably be so rapid in the foreseeable future that artificial organs will be better than the natural ones because there is no limit to what technology can accomplish!"

And so, let us now turn to the nuts and bolts of this business, to the actual devices and transplants that are creating bionic beings in growing and vast numbers each day.

PART II

Taking It From the Top: The Brain and the Head

Sci-fi itself hesitates to talk of artificial replacements or transplants for the brain. For even fiction recognizes the inviolability of that ultimate product of some four billion years of evolution. One automatically takes things from the top, though, and since the top of the human being is the head, let us start there. While an artificial brain, as Dr. Dobelle pointed out, is still far away from our current capabilities, scientists are implanting a wide range of devices into the brain and skull for a variety of purposes.

The reason for the difficulties of replacement or repair of the brain lie in that organ itself. Your brain consists of some 12 billion neurons, or nerve cells, plus another 100 billion glia cells, whose job is still unclear. On top of all this is the cerebral cortex—your brain's outer layer, the so-called gray matter—which performs the most complex of your thinking and other mental processes. About half the weight of the entire nervous system, your cortex is about one-tenth of an inch thick, a soft, wrinkled gray tissue, which stretched out would be some 3 feet long and 2 feet wide. A cubic inch of your brain contains about 100 million cells.

The neurons themselves have numerous fingers, or extensions, which reach out toward those of other neurons but never quite touch: they are separated from each other by a synapse, a space of less than one-millionth of an inch. When a message comes in (say, something you touched or heard or saw), it travels as a tiny burst of electricity along one of these fingers into the cell body. Then the neural, or nerve, impulse passes out along another finger to a synapse where this electrical impulse is converted into chemicals (neurotransmitters), which pour across the gap and set off another impulse in the next neuron to carry the message on its way, say from eye or ear to the brain's visual or auditory center. We know *what* happens in this process, but *how* it happens is still largely a mystery.

Synapses are one-way switches, police to control the constant enormous neural traffic in the brain. Synapses are so important that nature has built some 500 trillion of them into your brain, where some of the neurons possess almost a quarter of a million synapses each. Medical scientists are doing a lot of things to repair, check, and alter this amazing human organ, beginning with . . .

THE VERY TOP—SCALP AND SKULL

Right on top of it all is the scalp, the thin layer of skin on which your hair grows. And up here, doctors today are practicing transplantation for those who have lost their hair. Two hundred years ago, in the eighteenth century, was created an artificial replacement—the toupee (from the French word *toupet,* meaning tuft of hair), whose use today is said to be growing by leaps and bounds. A recent survey by the *The New York Times* reported that hair-piece orders in some stores had as much as tripled in the last three years and one dealer estimated that a million men now wear toupees, compared with some seventy-five thousand only twenty years earlier.

Doctors now actually transplant hair, using the recipient himself as a donor! A plug of scalp with perhaps a half-dozen hairs is taken from the back of the head where there is plenty and put into a hole prepared up front where the missing hair is most noticeable, and the transplant takes root there. It's all a little like moving plugs of grass around a lawn to cover the bare spots.

More vital and just as important to appearance is the replacement of lost parts of the skull, or cranium, the thick, strong, protective bone that shields and encloses your brain. Head injuries have always been common in war, but today's rising rate of sports and travel accidents has involved young people as never before. Such injuries, or brain surgery, may lead to loss or removal of large sections of the skull, leaving actual depressions where the brain is covered only by thin soft scalp tissue.

Doctors have been trying to cover such cranial gaps since J. van Meekren tried using a piece of dog bone for this purpose some three hundred years ago. He thus began an effort that is still being carried on with newer materials all the time. Those used have been either metals, such as lead, gold, silver, platinum, aluminum, stainless steel, chrome-cobalt alloys, and tantalum—or plastics, such as methylmethacrylate, polyethylene, and silicone rubber. Metal plates have certain drawbacks: X rays can't penetrate to allow doctors to check on brain conditions; the metal expands or contracts at a different rate than the bone in changing temperatures; and they must be fastened to the skull with screws or metal wires. Sometimes metal mesh is embedded in plastic and fastened in place with ordinary suture materials or wire to recreate the normal shape of the skull bones. Today's skull repairs are so effective that when one was dislodged after its young owner was hit right on the head with a baseball bat, all that had to be done was to reposition the plate and add some extra sutures to hold it in position.

BUGGING THE BRAIN AND OTHER BRAIN IMPLANTS

Normally there is a circulation of fluid through the spinal cord and brain tissue. Called cerebrospinal fluid (CSF), this acts as a shock absorber for the central nervous system (CNS—the brain and spinal cord) and probably also helps nourish the nerve tissues there as well. The CSF is a crystal-clear, watery-looking fluid constantly produced in the ventricles, the normal cavities of the brain. It circulates throughout the CNS and finally enters the bloodstream. Should this free flow or later absorption be impaired, the CSF will accumulate and build up pressure. Such a buildup of pressure may be caused by a brain tumor, hemorrhage, infection, birth defect, or an injury. When intracranial (inside the skull) pressure rises too high in a condition called hydrocephalus, or water on the brain, the head may be enlarged and the brain affected. The exact mechanism here is not really understood, but it is obvious that something has gone wrong with either the production or the absorption of this fluid.

When doctors want to measure this pressure and secure some CSF for checking, they insert a special hollow needle into the low back part of the spinal column—a spinal tap, or lumbar puncture. But now they also have a device less than half the size of a dime, which can be slipped through a small hole drilled directly in the skull and implanted under that bone to continuously monitor intracranial pressure.

This device has a pressure-sensitive membrane with a mounted mirror to reflect light back through three glass fibers. Changes in intracranial pressure move the mirror off center, causing the light to be reflected unevenly; a complex system outside the head then calculates the pressure. This implant allows doctors to check the pressure following injuries or surgery, or to diagnose hydrocephalus.

But this is not the only way that doctors monitor the brain to keep tabs on what is going on there. The brain's 12 billion neurons produce an electrical current of about one-ten-thousandth of a volt. These rhythmic fluctuations of voltage are known as *brain waves*, and these normally vary with the mind's activity—thinking, relaxing, sleeping, etc. The Alpha wave so widely discussed is just one of several brain waves. Doctors use these waves to diagnose disorders by measuring them with an instrument called an electroencephalograph, or an EEG.

An epileptic seizure, for example, has been shown to be a virtual electrical storm that sweeps over the brain. Often of unknown cause, epileptic seizures are preceded by special brain-wave patterns. This fact enables doctors to protect epileptics by attaching electrodes to the head and connecting these to a device small enough to fit in the pocket. The device monitors the electrical brain patterns and recognizes the pre-seizure brain waves: when these occur a buzzer goes off or a light flashes, giving the victim a warning to take the necessary medication or any other necessary precautions—stop driving, lie down, etc.

Doctors today are implanting devices in the brain to diagnose and relieve problems, to administer medication, and even to control behavior. For example, those suffering from hydrocephalus now have a tiny tube inserted to drain off the excessive CSF which might otherwise eventually lead to an enlarged head, mental retardation or other brain damage, invalidism, and even death.

Treatment today commonly consists of installing a plastic shunt with valves in a variety of forms. One is a flexible tube going from the distended brain ventricle through the veins all the way to the upper-right heart chamber, the atrium. Called a ventriculo-atrial (VA) shunt, this device allows excess CSF to drain directly into the bloodstream. Valves at the ends of the shunt control the flow of CSF so that a normal amount of fluid remains in the CNS. With one type of shunt a compressible sac about the size of a dime is placed directly under the scalp. This acts as a pumping device: should the shunt block up, one need only press down on the sac and it will blow out the blockage and reestablish drainage.

In other varieties of this shunt, the tube leads from the ventricle to empty into the chest outside the lungs, into the abdomen, or even into the ureter to be passed with the urine. Recently doctors have also introduced a shunt whose two ends are telescoped into the tube so that as the infant grows the shunt will also lengthen or "grow" and no surgery will be needed later in life to install a longer device.

Brain implants take other forms, too. At Roswell Park Memorial Institute, New York State's specialized cancer hospital in Buffalo, doctors are working with brain implants in a new attack on leukemia, that terrible killer of young people. Between 10 and 15 percent of those with leukemia develop this disease in the central nervous system, according to Dr. Arnold I. Freeman, Roswell Park's chief cancer-research pediatrician. But a brain implant now offers new hope.

A tiny bulblike device, the Ommaya reservoir, is implanted under the skin of the scalp. From this bulb a small tube passes directly into the cerebral ventricle, from which fluid drains into the spinal cord. Anticancer drugs are injected through the scalp into the Ommaya reservoir to pass through into the ventricles and then to the spinal cord. Dr. Freeman finds this method less painful than the old spinal taps used for this purpose and much more effective because it reduces the incidence of CNS leukemia by about two-thirds!

CONTROLLING THE BIONIC BRAIN

Barely a decade ago a Yale scientist, Dr. Jose Delgado, stood in a Cordoba bullring with a red cape and provoked an enraged bull into a wild charge. When the bull approached within a few feet of him, the scientist brought the animal to a dust-raising halt simply by pressing a button on a small device in his hand. Dr. Delgado had implanted electrodes in the animal's brain. A radio signal from his hand-held transmitter activated the electrodes in the bull's caudate nucleus, changing an angry, aggressive beast into a quiet, gentle one.

Such work with the emotions—anger, rage, etc.—has been done with animals by a variety of scientists. But other researchers have attempted to locate and stimulate the human pleasure center through implanted electrodes. Fixed to the skull bones and sometimes left in position for as long as three years, as many as 125 electrodes have been inserted into a single human brain. Such devices can be used to record the brain's electrical activity during

31

normal or abnormal episodes, during relaxation or intense emotions. In some instances the patients themselves have carried a control box with which they activated electrodes in their brains, thus stimulating their pleasure centers to overcome otherwise uncontrollable pain, anger, or anxiety.

Clearly we have taken our first halting steps toward that distant goal of an artificial brain, or control over the natural organ's function. For example, Dr. Lawrence R. Pinneo and his associates at California's Stanford Research Institute have developed a method for restoring lost control over a monkey's paralyzed limbs. They implanted electrodes in the area of the brain that controlled the movements of the paralyzed limb.

The Stanford scientists then used a computer to develop patterns of activating the electrodes to stimulate cerebral neurons in such a way as to produce purposeful movement in the paralyzed arm. One computer program made the monkey reach out for food and carry it to its mouth; another pattern caused the arm to stretch out for climbing; and still another had it scratch the animal's back. Finally, the Stanford team even provided a set of switches so the monkey could select its own program to produce desired movements.

Other investigators have succeeded in applying similar principles to human beings. In the past five years, neurosurgeons have taken up the so-called cerebellar stimulator developed by Dr. Irving S. Cooper of New York Medical College and some seven hundred of these devices have been implanted. The stimulators consist of a silicone-coated mesh plate with four to eight pairs of platinum electrodes attached to a part of the brain called the cerebellum, which controls muscular coordination. These electrodes can be activated to stimulate the cerebellum through an antenna placed under the skin of the chest. A battery-powered transmitter, small enough to fit into the patient's pocket, allows the patient to turn the stimulator on and off as desired. These devices are often called brain pacemakers because the first of this family of electronic devices was the famous and widely used heart pacemaker, which we will discuss in Part III.

These cerebellar stimulators can be thought of as electronic brain assisters. They have been tried for a number of conditions—cerebral palsy, epilepsy, and other spastic muscular conditions. They are reported to have helped, for example, a 12-year-old boy with cerebral palsy who was unable to sit by himself, and others who couldn't feed themselves or operate their own wheel-chairs. The best results with these devices are reported among the younger patients, who, thanks to the stimulators, do things not otherwise possible.

The stimulating electrical pulses of these devices may be applied for ten-minute periods in each waking hour or simply used on and off around the clock. The costs are considerable: roughly $5,000 for the device and the operation necessary to implant electrodes and receiver, and another $10,000 for hospitalization costs. Although the demand for such devices currently runs high, a very recent meeting of experts in rehabilitation medicine voiced some doubts about the method's efficacy and long-term safety. The general feeling at the meeting was that stricter and more objective studies of these implantations are needed.

Electrical stimulation has also been tried for control of pain. Less than a decade ago scientists tried implanting electrodes in the center of the cerebral cortex of rats: stimulating the area electrically made these animals immune to pain. Neurosurgeons have since tried implanting electrodes in the human thalamus (the part of the brain that relays sensation to the cortex) to help patients suffering from constant, uncontrollable pain. This seems to work, and these sufferers turn their stimulators on as they feel the need for pain relief. But electronic pain control is still so new that it must be regarded as experimental. Further along, however, is another type of implant in the head . . .

ARTIFICIAL EYES AND EYE IMPLANTS

Artificial eyes are part of man's earliest history. These devices were already old when the *Rig-Veda,* the ancient Hindu book of knowledge, recorded their use some thirty-five hundred years ago. About that same time, the early Egyptians were making artificial eyes of wax or even plaster. Mankind has used an incredible range of materials for this purpose—wood, ivory, bone, precious and mineral stones, seashells, even gold and silver. But glass eyes were first made by the Venetians in 1579. At first these were simply oval shells, ill-fitting and uncomfortable. French surgeons of the seventeenth and nineteenth centuries were the first to make modern types of glass eyes.

Before 1939 virtually all artificial eyes used in the United States were fashioned from imported German glass. When the German eye-makers' guild restricted exports and raised prices, American manufacturers developed glass of a comparable quality. And after World War II, most "glass eyes" were actually made of plastic and surgeons began to develop artificial eyes that were actually implanted into the orbit instead of simply being slipped into place as was previously done. Techniques were devised to attach the muscles that normally move the natural eye to the implant so the artificial eye would tend to move just as the natural one did.

Newest and still controversial is a magnetic eye widely used in Great Britain. This consists of two plastic halves or hemispheres, each of which has embedded in it a tiny rectangular magnet. The inner half is surgically implanted in the orbit and attached to the eye muscles. It is covered with eye tissue (the conjunctiva) and entirely buried. When this has fully healed, the outer half with its pupil and visible parts is inserted so the two magnets are opposite each other and separated only by the thin conjunctival tissue. Young patients are seen twice yearly to be given larger eyes to keep pace with their growth. Some find magnetic eyes move much as the natural ones do.

Eye structures such as pupil and iris are handpainted in oils on the final acrylic eyes, and individual colorings and tiny veins of almost microscopic red thread are applied. This artistry is then sealed under a final outer layer of transparent plastic to retain its appearance. In those rare instances when a person is allergic to the plastic, the old glass eyes may be used.

We have already seen how earlier doctors struggled with a whole flock of different materials and methods in their attempts to replace damaged corneas before succeeding with a transplant in an antelope a century and a half ago. But modern human corneal transplants have only really been successful on any meaningful scale since World War II. Because the cornea has no blood supply it is safe from rejection, but both recipient eye and donor cornea must be healthy and in good condition. It's now possible to freeze-dry corneas donated to the Eye Bank. These are passed through several solutions and then frozen in liquid nitrogen at -196° C. (roughly

-325° F.). Corneal transplantation is a surgical miracle of delicate precision, typically performed by a surgeon using a microscope to see and work more accurately.

The same surgical trephine—a sort of medical cookie-cutter—is used to remove the desired donor cornea and the recipient's own diseased one so that the donor plug will fit precisely into the recipient eye. The corneal plug is generally 6 to 9 mm. (roughly two-tenths to three-eighths of an inch). Once placed in position, this may be sutured there with sixteen to twenty-four separate stitches, which are generally removed seven to ten weeks later. The current success rate of expert corneal surgeons runs 80 to 90 percent and is steadily improving.

Mankind has always sought to improve or save vision. Cataracts, a clouding of the eye's lens, interfering with sight, were treated surgically in India three thousand years ago, much as they are today. Those ancients also removed the cataractous lens. They, however, did this by poking the lens so it fell back inside the eyeball, while today's surgeons lift it out. Of course, once the lens is removed, light is not adequately focused on the retina, where images are formed and nerve cells send the message of what is seen back to the brain's visual center.

Replacing the lost lens with eyeglasses is a problem, for these act like magnifying lenses, enlarging the size of objects by 20 to 35 percent and distorting the edges. Contact lenses are a distinct improvement with only a 6 percent enlargement, but the patient must wait six weeks to three months for these to be fitted. However, World War II opened a new world of cataract vision with implant lenses.

Many British airmen in that war had pieces of their plastic plane windows blasted into their eyes by German gunfire. British ophthalmologist Harold Ridley was amazed to find that this material, methylmethacrylate, produced no irritation. So he developed and inserted the first plastic intraocular lens implant to replace the removed cataractous lens. Early poor design and crude surgery led to many failures, but other European doctors tried a host of different approaches. Some even used tooth material with a center of clear plastic glued into the eye with dental cement.

In the early 1960s Dr. Cornelius D. Binkhorst, a Dutch ophthalmologist, was the first to really succeed with these lens implants. He clipped his improved models directly to the iris, the colored part of the eye, utilizing advanced surgical techniques. With this lens implant, the enlargement of objects is only 3 percent and patients find they either need no eyeglasses at all or simple ones with mildly corrective lenses such as those any normal eye might need. One of our own leading experts—Dr. Norman S. Jaffee of the University of Miami—recently estimated that there are more than forty thousand such implants in place and some seventy-five hundred are being inserted each year.

PART III

The Bionic Person Turns Electronic

NATURE LEADS THE WAY

Electricity and electronics are usually regarded as the hallmark of our Space Age, and most people think the use of electrical devices in medicine is strictly the stuff of today. But that really isn't so! People have been using electricity in medicine for five thousand years at the very least. And nature herself has utilized electricity by evolving powerful biological batteries in several families of fish. These electrical organs can produce as much as 1,000 volts (your house current is 110), enough to knock down a man, or even a horse.

Groping his way along in nature's footsteps, man has only recently managed to devise and implant in the human body a variety of electrical devices. With these electronic marvels doctors can stimulate the brain and the spinal cord, and produce artificial eyes and ears, making these devices do the job of the natural organs.

But nature's own electricity—termed bioelectricity by scientists—is actually inherent in virtually all living creatures and is as universal as table salt, sodium chloride. As we've discussed earlier, such bioelectricity is produced when your brain cells work (the brain waves); it travels along nerves to transmit their messages; and muscles produce it when they contract. Certain fish—electric eels, catfish, and rays—produce sizable amounts of electricity in highly specialized structures called electric organs. In these creatures, nature has modified muscular tissue and converted it into disk-shaped flattened cells called electroplaques. These cells are piled in stacks, connected in series, like storage batteries. Somehow, in a way not yet really understood, these organs break down body chemicals, converting the energy thus released into electricity.

The most powerful of these fish is the electric eel, which can reach 8 or 9 feet in length and be as thick around as a man's thigh. The tail region comprises about four-fifths of the entire body length and contains this fish's electric organ in the form of columns or stacks of disk-shaped cells. This organ produces an electrical current running from its electrically positive tail end to its negative front end. This unique fish delivers its most powerful shock when its head and tail are in contact with widely separated spots on the body of its victim.

The electric eel can actually deliver a shock of 600 to 1,000 volts. The chief purpose of such electricity is to paralyze the eel's prey—and the shock is enough to stun creatures up to the size of a man or a horse. Exhibitors of these fish often set up a whole row of electric bulbs attached to the fish tank so that whenever the eel discharges its electricity, the bulbs light up.

The electric catfish, on the other hand, grows to 4 feet in length, but it can still deliver a good-sized electrical wallop of up to 450 volts. This fish, a native of tropical Africa, uses its electricity chiefly for defense or for the capture of its prey. Finally, there are the electric rays, or torpedoes, which grow to no more than 6 feet in length and can deliver up to 80 volts, quite enough to knock a man down. The torpedo inhabits the seas of the warm or temperate climates, such as the shores of Italy or Greece.

Ancient man must surely have been aware of the presence of such bizarre electrical developments, for these fish inhabited the very seas which lapped the shores of many of our earliest civilizations, such as the Egyptian, Grecian, and Roman. It seems that the knowledge and use of the shocks delivered by the electric catfish were already old when the early Egyptians carefully included drawings of these fish in the murals adorning a number of their ancient tombs. And in ancient Pompeii a mosaic floor dating back two thousand years has a torpedo pictured on it.

Aristotle and Plato, some twenty-five hundred years ago, were both aware that the electric ray was quite capable of numbing any human arm or leg it touched. But the first recorded medical use of this electricity came at about the time of Jesus. It was then that Anthero, a Roman freedman plagued by gout, stepped on an electric ray while walking along those ancient Italian shores. The sting numbed his leg, and when the numbness had passed, so had the pain of his gout. Following this incident, a Roman physician, Scribonius Largus, began advising a new headache remedy: the application of a torpedo with its electric shock to the head. He also recommended the fish to gout sufferers, who were advised to apply it to the aching foot until the leg was numb clear up to the knee.

At that same time, Pedanius Dioscorides—a famous Greek physician and surgeon to Nero's armies—wrote his classic *Materia Medica,* a treatise on every form of medical remedy then known. This became the ultimate authority for all treatment and was followed by physicians for the next fifteen hundred years. In it, Dioscorides touted the use of these electric fish for headache, gout, diseases of the spleen, and intestinal conditions. Such medical use of electricity was followed well into the Middle Ages. In fact, many primitive African tribes still employ the electric catfish and its shocks for just such medicinal purposes.

And we still follow surprisingly similar practices today. Modern scientific medicine uses electrical stimulation and shocks in a wide variety of ways: those we have seen in Part II, and the implantation of electrical devices to produce sight and hearing, to conquer pain and straighten curved backs, to control the effects of multiple sclerosis, and to make tissues heal. There are implanted devices to monitor bones and teeth; and similar devices make it possible to monitor women in labor. And many people depend on other electrical equipment to keep their heart and lungs functioning.

THE MIRACLE OF ARTIFICIAL SIGHT

The Gallup organization recently conducted a poll of Americans and found that, with the sole exception of cancer, blindness is more feared than any other affliction. And with 1 million Americans unable to read a newspaper even with the help of eyeglasses, and some 500,000 blind, the possibility of artificial sight becomes tremendously important, a major achievement for all time when it has been ultimately perfected.

To achieve success with artificial vision, we must first understand how the normal eye functions. It all begins with light striking the eye. This light is focused by the cornea and the lens of the eye onto the back wall of the eyeball where the retina is stretched. This tissue is onionskin thin—some 0.2 mm., less than one-hundredth of an inch—and barely the size of a postage stamp, less than a square inch in surface. The retina contains by some estimates over 150 million photoreceptors, cells that respond to light. But you actually "see" at the very back of your brain, for this remarkable organ must take the upside-down images that the lens focuses on the retina, and the two different images seen by your right and left eyes, and come up with a single meaningful right-side-up picture of the world you view.

To get the image back to the visual center of your brain, the retina sends nerve messages racing through the neurons of the optic nerve at the incredible rate of 300 miles an hour to the back of your brain. There the visual cortex deals with these nerve impulses (essentially electrical ones) and interprets them or sends them on to deeper parts of the brain for further interpretation or processing. This is why a blow on the back of the head causes you to "see stars" for if the blow is strong enough, it stimulates the visual center, which reacts by reporting or "seeing" dots of light, what scientists call phosphenes. Scientists are now utilizing this reaction to help the blind to "see" again!

It is possible for doctors actually to monitor individual neurons in the visual cortex. But the complexity of this task is clear from the fact that millions of nerve fibers pour into this center, where they connect with others. However, specific neurons respond to different retinal stimulation. Thus, one such cortical neuron might react to a line or a bar shown to the eye or to a rectangle that moves upward, but not to one moving sideways. Each neuron is very specific, reacting only to a particular shape, position, or movement. From just such knowledge will come the artificial sight of the future.

Dr. Dobelle credits the original idea of electronic sight to our own Benjamin Franklin. It wasn't until the 1950s, however, that an American researcher patented a device to produce and send electronic signals to the visual center to produce phosphenes, or spots of light. But the electronic wizardry, the miniaturized circuitry and transistors, and the means of programming such stimulation were not then available. Then, in 1968, it all came together at the University of London when Dr. Giles M. Brindley, a neurophysiologist and expert in electronic engineering, produced artificial sight in a blind woman.

A neurosurgeon cut a small hole (roughly 1½ inches) in her skull, through which were fed eighty electronic wires to actually contact the visual cortex. A set of eighty radio receivers encased in a silicone cap was buried between the scalp and the cranial bones, while eighty transmitters were put in a hat the woman could wear. Of these eighty electrodes, thirty-seven produced spots of light which the patient saw when the doctors sent electrical stimuli through the electrodes. The subject perceived an effect not unlike that of a theater marquee, where various bulbs are lit to be seen as numbers, words, or simple objects. It was all very crude, but it did work and did prove that artificial sight is possible and in the not-too-distant future.

In 1969 Dr. Kolff and Dr. Dobelle at the University of Utah began to expand and refine Brindley's work. Dr. Dobelle headed a team that traveled around the United States and Canada to some sixty neurosurgery hospital services, observing brain operations that exposed the visual cortexes of some thirty-seven people. Between 1970 and 1974 this team learned a great deal about how the visual cortex actually works through trials on such cooperating patients. There could be no doubt now that stimulating an electrode on the visual cortex produces a point of light, a phosphene. Adjacent electrodes, however, may produce phosphenes seen as quite far apart in the visual field of any person, and the phosphenes produced by stimulating the same spot on the visual cortex in different people may be "seen" in quite different places.

By 1974 Dr. Dobelle and his team were implanting a grid of sixty-four electrodes on the visual cortex. They plotted the spot where the subject saw the phosphene each time an electrode was stimulated, say in the upper right-hand corner, in the center, close to one another, or far away. This knowledge was programmed into a massive computer connected to the electronic cortical implant. The computer could plan the phosphenes to produce a visual pattern in the mind of the subject such that he would "see," for example, the six dots that compose a particular Braille letter and could thus read Braille by sight instead of touch.

One 28-year-old veteran, blinded in combat, was thus able to recognize a triangle being shown him, perceive that it was pointing upward, and even identify letters, shapes, and patterns. The electrodes, however, were still being implanted on a temporary basis and were removed after the trials.

Then came the ultimate test. The patient was a 33-year-old man blinded in an accident some ten years earlier. A small piece of bone (typically, 2-by-3 inches) was removed from the rear of his skull, and an array of sixty-four electrodes embedded in a thin strip of Teflon was placed over the visual cortex. A TV camera was pointed at an object, and the image was then sent to the computer, which stimulated the appropriate electrodes in the patient's brain. Connecting electrical wires from these electrodes were slipped under the scalp to a spot over the right ear where a device the size of a dime protruded through the skin. Virtually an electric plug, not unlike a wall plug, the wires from the controlling computer were plugged in here.

The computer then mapped out on a TV screen the spot where each electrode produced a phosphene in relation to the others. Using this system, the young man was able to read Braille at thirty characters a minute without practice—five times faster than he could read with his fingertips. With the TV camera, the blind man was also able to detect white horizontal and vertical lines on a dark background.

Dr. Kolff is extremely enthusiastic about the future applications of this work: "With this we believe we have demonstrated the future potential of the artificial eye . . . we hope that eventually we will be able to produce a mobility prosthesis . . . a device that will enable a blind man to get around without bumping into objects or other people."

Dr. Dobelle refuses to say anything is impossible, and his concept is truly one for the bionic person. He foresees the use of a glass eye with a lens and a miniaturized camera actually implanted in the eye socket and attached to the eye muscles. A wire from this camera would transmit the levels of light in the viewed object to an eyeglass frame housing a tiny computer; this would then convert the light into electricity to be carried through the scalp to electrodes permanently implanted on the visual cortex.

And now to the next step in the developing bionic people . . .

THE BIONIC EAR

When sound waves enter your outer ear, they beat on a drum (the eardrum or tympanic membrane), which separates the outer air and world from the middle ear. In this chamber, the middle ear, are three bones so tiny that all of them could be held simultaneously on the tip of your little finger. One—the stapes, or stirrup—is the smallest bone in the human body. Sound waves cause these bones to vibrate and so transmit sound to the inner ear with its cochlea (which means "snail shell" and looks like one).

Fluid in the inner ear transmits these vibrations through the cochlea, which contains thousands of sensory or receptor cells, each of which has microscopic hairs projecting into the fluid. The vibrations of this inner-ear fluid move the cochlear cell hairs. This movement sets off electrical or neural impulses which are carried by the cochlear nerve to the brain, where they are interpreted as hearing. The ear thus changes sound waves into electrical nerve signals, which the hearing, or auditory, brain center "hears" as words, music, or other sounds, much as the retina and visual cortex "see" with light.

But hearing, too, may be damaged or lost. A 17-year-old had his snowmobile souped up for racing by putting on a straight-pipe exhaust and increasing engine compression, making it both faster and much noisier. After five years of driving this machine he complained of a ringing in his ears; tests revealed a permanent loss of hearing from all this noise.

We've come a long way from the ear trumpet with its large mouth and narrow tip fitting into the outer ear, yet this was the earliest and only hearing aid until this

47

century. Then came the various electrical and electronic devices that amplified sound. These were used in the outer ear to transmit an increased sound vibration to the eardrum, or placed against the bone behind the ear to transmit the vibrations to the skull, where these vibrations were picked up by the nerves and transmitted to the auditory center.

Scientists are now planning and testing a whole new world of artificial hearing for those who cannot hear with any conventional aids. Dr. Richard Goode, an ear specialist at Stanford University Medical Center in California, is working on a device he hopes will soon be totally implantable within the head. All that's needed to make this a reality is a small rechargeable battery the size of a quarter. This system calls for placement of a tiny magnet on the eardrum or the ear bones: a tiny amplifier and microphone are used to pick up the sounds and convert them to electromagnetic waves. These waves move the magnet, thus vibrating the eardrum or bones to produce the sensation of sound. Believed to be only a few years off and totally implantable, this device would provide a marked improvement in the quality of hearing and would have the added advantage of being invisible.

The truly bionic person will surely be able to have artificial hearing through one of two methods now being tested: either through electrodes implanted directly into the cochlea or through electrodes in the auditory cortex. This involves a sort of pedestal behind the ear for connection to some source of electrical stimulation, such as a computer, for experimental testing. Or a receiver may be totally buried under the skin with an electronic button placed on the skin overlying this receiver. The button— not unlike those used for conventional hearing aids—is connected by electrical wires to a pocket device no larger than a cigarette package, which picks up and converts sound into electrical radio impulses. These are then transmitted through the skin to electrodes in the cochlea.

While these cochlear implant hearing devices cannot restore the kind of hearing experienced with the normal ear, most people using these devices find them helpful in a variety of ways. The patients wearing the devices were better at lip reading, the intelligibility of their own speech increased, and most were able to identify such common sounds as the telephone ringing. One man would call his wife from the office and get a yes or no answer to a question by having her answer in an agreed upon one- or two-syllable word: one syllable would mean "yes" and the other "no," for although he couldn't distinguish specific words, he was able to distinguish the number of syllables.

Experiments using electrodes on the auditory cortex are less advanced, and this research is still too undeveloped to provide any real information from those who view it as the eventual alternative to cochlear implants.

But the ear isn't the only organ that can be helped in this way. There's a whole other world of electronic devices for the rest of the body.

THE AMAZING PACEMAKERS: HEART, SPINE, AND DIAPHRAGM

The human heart beats about seventy times a minute, an elephant's some thirty-five, and a mouse's races at about five hundred. During heavy exercise your normal heart rate may nearly double. Your heart is controlled, or paced, by a tiny lump of modified muscle at the back of its right side, the sinoatrial node. Medical scientists still don't quite understand just how this natural pacemaker works. But anything that damages this vital bit of tissue, such as a heart attack, or interferes with the conduction of its signal will disturb the rate at which the heart pumps and make it either irregular or too slow. Such abnormal functioning can cost the victim his life or make him a half-cripple unable to perform his normal activities. Such disturbances can sometimes be congenital, present at birth.

The solution to this problem has been a miracle in a battery, the heart pacemaker, probably the most successful electronic device ever implanted in the human body. These devices have been put into nearly half a million people around the world—from a 26-hour-old premature infant to patients in their 90s. Essentially these cardiac (heart) pacemakers restore and maintain the proper rhythm of the heart beat by substituting their electrical shocks—minute, painless, and 0.867 seconds apart—for the natural pacemaker's maintenance of rhythmic heart action.

Today these systems are so sophisticated that the so-called demand pacers act only when the heart itself fails to beat on schedule. When the heart is beating normally, the battery powering the pacer shuts itself off and preserves its strength while avoiding interfering with the natural heart rhythm. Most commonly, the whole thing is implanted with local anesthesia (the kind of injection a dentist gives to drill a tooth painlessly). The battery is installed in a space created under the skin, usually near the armpit. Then the plastic-coated electrode wire is passed through veins until it comes to rest in the heart, where its bare metal tip contacts the heart muscle itself. Sometimes, however, the chest is opened and the device put into place with its electrode stitched to the heart itself. In fact, some doctors are now actually using a special corkscrew tip to screw the electrode directly into the heart muscle.

The big problem with pacemakers has been the batteries, which until recently had to be changed at least every couple of years. Today doctors have a choice of devices—there are even nuclear pacemakers available. The latest variety of nuclear pacemaker battery is powered by plutonium-238 and should last forty years or more. It is safe from a radiation point of view: the owners will get less radiation than that permitted in occupational exposures; and the immediate family will get an amount roughly one-twenty-fifth of the average annual exposure we all get from natural background radiation.

Now, too, a team from Pennsylvania State University has implanted a device with a life of twenty years or more for its silicon-mercury-zinc battery, which can function without recharging for three years or more. Only a half-inch thick and about the size of a double lipstick case, the unit is recharged by simply holding an electronic device on the skin over the battery for about forty-five minutes.

These cardiac pacemakers opened a whole new world of similar devices in a broad range of applications, from Dr. Cooper's brain pacemakers described in Part II to those now used to control intractable, incapacitating and uncontrollable pain.

The dorsal column stimulator (DCS) was the first of these pain-control devices to follow on the heels of the heart pacemaker. The first DCS was installed in a patient in 1967. This is the basic procedure: a window the size of a quarter is first cut into the spine. Then a bit of silastic plastic holding three platinum electrodes is slipped in to lie on the spinal cord itself, separated from it by only the thinnest of tissue. Stainless steel wires run from the spinal electrodes under the skin to a radio-frequency (RF) receiver the size of a man's wristwatch. The receiver is commonly planted below the ribcage and on a line with the arm. To the skin over this is taped a doughnut-shaped plastic antenna, whose radio signals come from a higher-powered transmitter the size of a cigarette package and carried in a pocket or on the belt. The device delivers a pulsating electrical current to the spine, and this sometimes eliminates the pain. Sufferers can turn the device on and off as they wish, and raise its power to as much as 25 volts. It gives a buzzing or tingling sensation that can make the pain bearable for some.

Very similar to the DCS is the carotid nerve stimulator. Angina pectoris (literally a severe pain in the chest) is a heart condition in which there is severe and often incapacitating chest pain. Electrodes placed about the carotid sinus nerves in each side of the neck are connected to an RF receiver implanted under the clavicle, or collar bone. An antenna placed on the skin over the receiver transmits radio signals from a transmitter in the patient's pocket or on the belt. The pain of the angina—commonly triggered by strenuous physical activity or very cold weather—can usually be brought to an end by activating the stimulator.

Phrenic nerve stimulators are similar to both these devices. These are often used to help quadriplegics, many of whom are in their teens, victims of injury to the spinal cord from sports accidents. The phrenic nerve controls the diaphragm and thus the respiratory rate. There are also disorders that affect the respiratory center in the brain. During sleep such sufferers who breathe normally during the day may literally forget to breathe.

Older treatment for such patients utilized mechanical respirators once called iron lungs. Now, however, electrodes are placed on the two phrenic nerves, and separate receivers are placed on the two sides of the chest. During the day the patient must move the antenna from one to the other because after twelve to eighteen hours of constant stimulation the nerve is fatigued. Quadriplegics use a transmitter that is not battery-powered but is simply plugged into the house electrical current.

These noncardiac pacemakers have been successfully used for a variety of problems with varying success. Scoliosis is the side-to-side spinal curvature that is particularly noticeable in young children and teenagers. Using what is virtually a modified cardiac pacemaker, the spinal muscles are stimulated so that the spine straightens itself out. However, it always takes time to find out whether such results are worthwhile and lasting. Treatment is usually started with youngsters. The first such patient was an 8-year-old.

From a receiver the size of a silver dollar, wires run to a number of electrodes placed on the muscles on the convex side of the spinal curvature. The doughnut-shaped antenna is placed on the skin over the receiver and is powered by a cigarette-pack-sized transmitter. The stimulation consists of electric pulses throughout the night, and there are no limitations on the daily activity or lifestyle of the young person. When the spine straightens out, the device is no longer used.

With more than 125,000 spinal-injured paraplegic patients in the United States alone, their problems demand recognition. One of the most distressing is the loss of the ability to urinate as a result of nerve-control destruction. Pacemakers have been brought to the aid of such people, too. Implanting these devices in the bladder wall in one method, or on the appropriate nerves in the lower end of the spinal cord in another, has shown that it is possible for these sufferers to gain control of this function. With such pacemakers in position, they can achieve bladder control by activating the pacemaker as needed, thus substituting electrical stimulation for lost nerve impulses and bringing us one step closer to the reality of the Six Million Dollar Man.

HEALING WITH ELECTRICITY— GROWING NEW LIMBS?

Dr. Robert O. Becker, a professor of orthopedics at the State University of New York, recently affirmed his opinion: "I believe that by effecting the proper hormone balance and using electricity, we can produce regeneration." Since making that statement, he has succeeded in obtaining some limb regeneration or regrowth in rats and frogs, which do not normally regenerate such missing parts. Bone, cartilage, muscle, nerves, and even blood vessels were all regenerated by this electrical stimulation. The electricity needed is small, but the amount must be precise: in rats, three- to six-billionths of an ampere is needed—a car battery by comparison may use 6 amperes.

Doctors have shown that skin ulcers heal better when low-intensity direct current is applied to the wound. Others have found that inserting an electrode directly into a nonhealing fracture or broken bone will induce healing or speed up the process. The really thrilling stories are those of children and young adults who have had their legs saved from amputation: repeated operations failed to produce healing of broken shin bones, but electricity or electromagnetic treatments induced healing without further surgery.

The medical uses of electricity are truly fantastic, but perhaps the most interesting application concerns . . .

BUGGING THE BODY

We've already seen how the brain is monitored, but in fact such electronic bugging is done all over the body. Monitoring devices have even been implanted in living teeth: a miniaturized radio transmitter (consisting of a mercury battery and multi-layered switch) small enough to fit into a natural tooth has been implanted in one jaw so that when the switch contacts the teeth in the opposite jaw, tooth contacts and jaw movements can be monitored by tuning in on the resulting transmission.

Dr. Timothy J. Kriewall, professor of bioengineering at the University of Michigan, has contrived a device to tune in on childbirth. The appliance consists of a tiny magnet, which is attached to one edge of the cervix (the opening of the uterus). Opposite the magnet on the circumference of the cervix, an equally small magnetic sensor is attached. As the cervix dilates to begin the process of childbirth, the sensor picks up electromagnetic waves and passes them on to measuring instruments outside the body. In this way the obstetrician can follow the progress of the birth.

And then there's the "telltale nail" devised by Dr. Victor H. Frankel, then professor of orthopedic surgery at Case Western Reserve. Broken bones are held together with nails during healing. Dr. Frankel's nail contained an AM-FM radio transmitter, a strain gauge and battery, and even an on-off switch operated from outside the body by an ordinary magnet. The broadcast tone rises as pressure on the hip and nail increases. This tells doctors about the strains exerted on broken hips during movement and nursing care, enabling them to ensure better medical care in the future.

These devices are all part and parcel of today's very real bionic people—the ones that are here, right now. Let us look at the nuts and bolts, the joints and muscles of this bionic person.

Artificial vision of the future: glass eye with lens and camera transmits light to a computer built into eyeglass frame. The computer translates light into an electric current, which is carried to electrodes implanted on the brain.

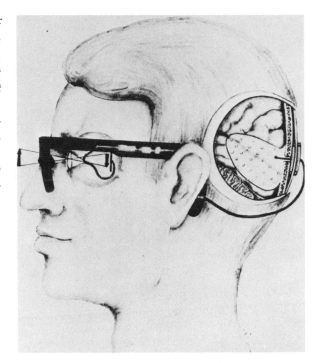

X ray shows sixty-four platinum electrodes in a Teflon matrix implanted on the visual cortex of the brain. Future system will use many more electrodes.

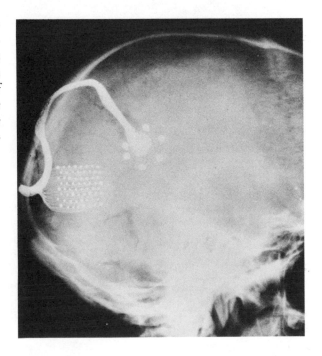

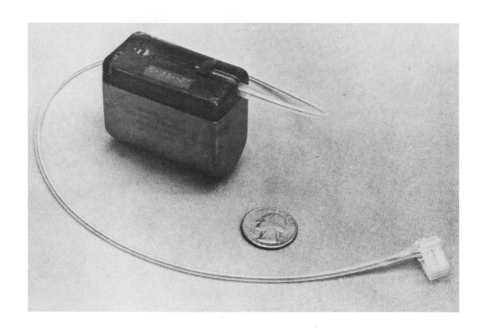

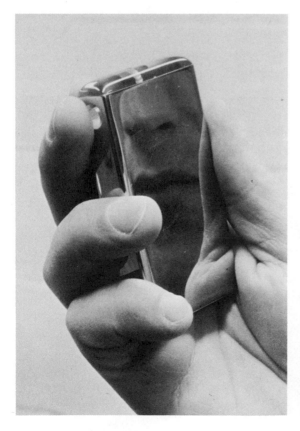

Heart patients could use this plutonium-powered pacemaker for at least forty years, longer than the lifespan of most recipients.

The long-life, rechargeable Penn State-Hershey pacemaker, implanted in nine patients in the last two years, is held by cardiothoracic surgeon Dr. G. Frank O. Tyers, one of its inventors.

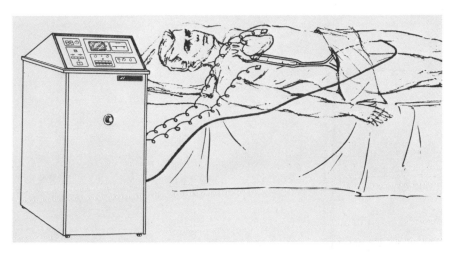

This intra-aortic balloon pump eases the workload of the heart's left ventricle, which pumps blood. The pump increases and decreases pressure in the aorta, the main channel from the heart to the rest of the body.

The intra-aortic pump consists of a 10-inch long, ¾-inch diameter balloon with a thin gas tube running down its center. An external unit operates the balloon in synchronism with the heart. Using a local anesthetic, the surgeon inserts the balloon pump into the femoral artery in the thigh, and then threads it into the aorta.

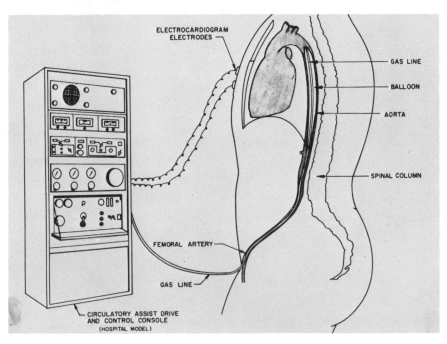

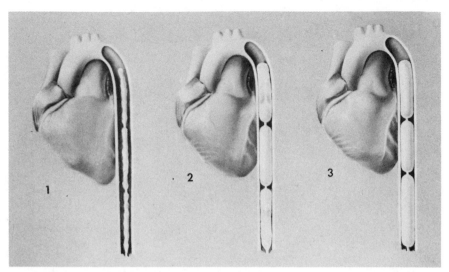

The intra-aortic pump operates in this way: (1) The heart contracts, pumping blood into the aorta. The balloon deflates. (2) The heart begins to relax; the aortic valve is closed. The balloon expands, forcing blood into both the upper and lower body. (3) The heart is fully relaxed, the balloon fully inflated. As the heart begins its next cycle, the balloon deflates, leaving a low-pressure area into which the heart easily pumps.

The balloon portion of the intra-aortic balloon pump is available in five different sizes. It can be used for children, teenagers, and adults.

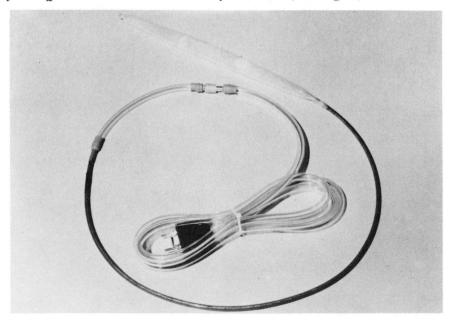

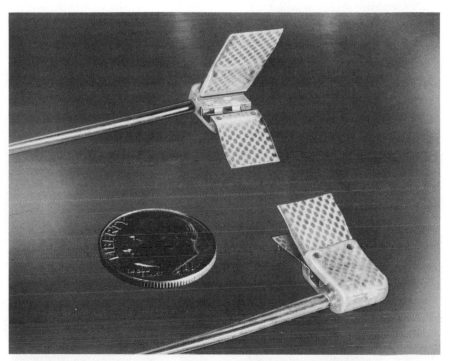

The carotid sinus nerve stimulator, shown above and below, is about the size of a dime.

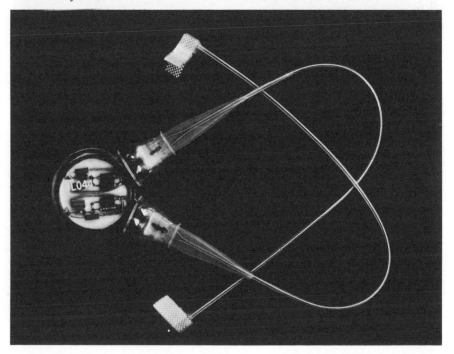

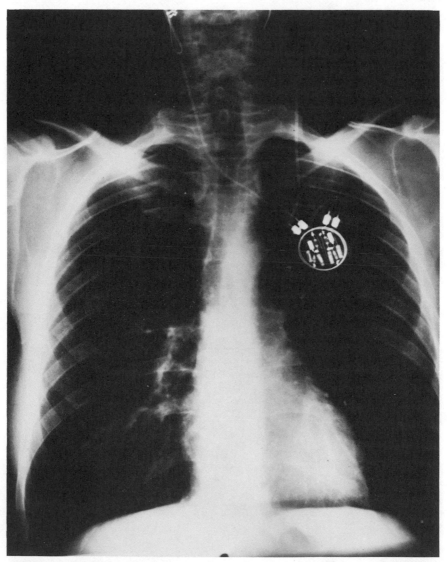

X-ray photo shows electrodes attached to the carotid sinus nerves in both sides of the neck. These electrodes connect to a receiver implanted under the skin of the chest. Patient can end severe chest pain by activating the stimulator.

This total shoulder pros-
thesis, possibly the first
successful American de-
sign for shoulder replacement, was developed by
a team of orthopedic sur-
geons at Chicago's Mi-
chael Reese Medical
Center.

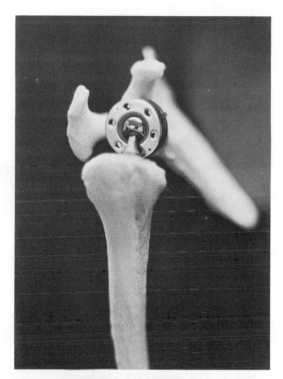

The total artificial shoulder is held against a
normal shoulder to show
its placement. The pros-
thesis has been implanted
in numerous patients
with good results.

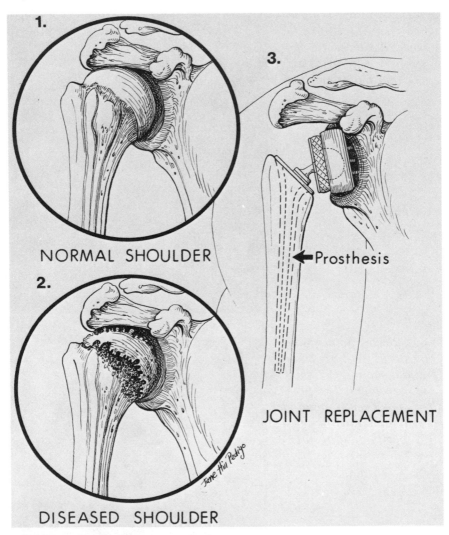

1.

NORMAL SHOULDER

2.

DISEASED SHOULDER

3.

←Prosthesis

JOINT REPLACEMENT

The first sketch shows a normal shoulder bone joint, and the second its deterioration from disease. The third sketch depicts the new artificial shoulder and bone joint in place.

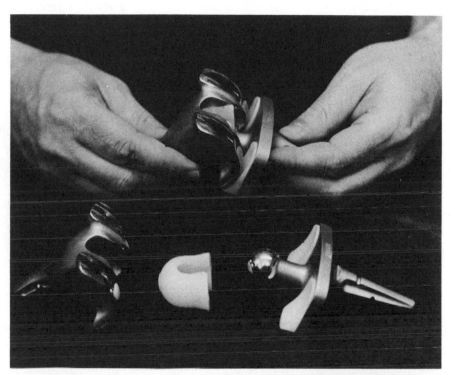

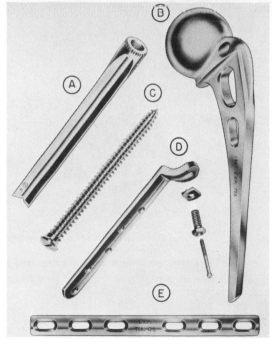

The spherocentric artificial knee developed at the University of Michigan is shown assembled in a 90° angle of flex. The disassembled parts rest on the table.

Surgical implants made from titanium are shown: (A) hip nail; (B) hip prosthesis; (C) hip screw; (D) intertrochanteric plate; and (E) slotted pattern plate.

As part of a research program on an artificial muscle, Dr. Kenneth E. Hughes attaches a strain gauge to the muscle to monitor its tension.

This ceramic tooth root has been used successfully in animals. Top photo shows a ceramic and metallic tooth assembly that is under evaluation. After the root is secured in the jaw, a conventional tooth crown is placed on the post. Bottom photo is an X ray taken at eighteen months. It shows the bone growth that takes place around the root, filling in the jagged edges.

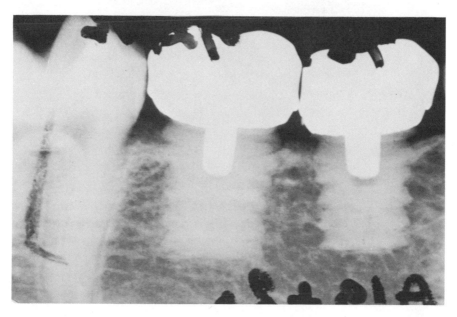

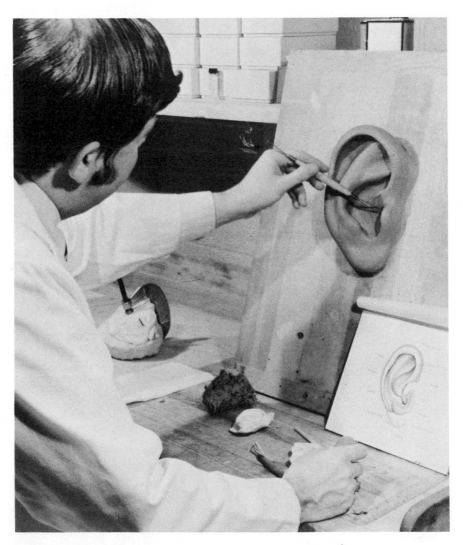

Professor Denis C. Lee of the University of Michigan Medical School sculpts clay (above) to prepare a teaching model for plastic surgery. A plastic model will be made from a mold of the clay, and then colored. On facing page (top), Professor Lee removes an ear prosthesis (artificial ear) from a mold. Below, he tints the ear to match the patient's coloring.

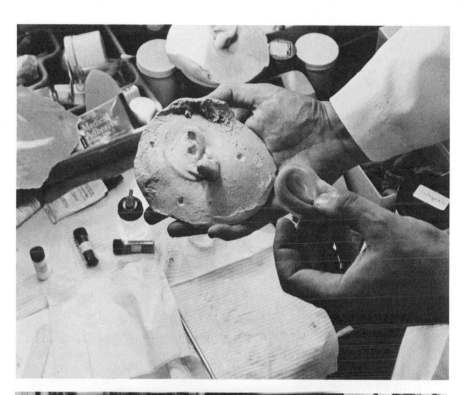

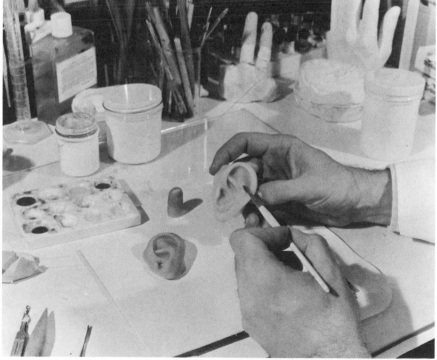

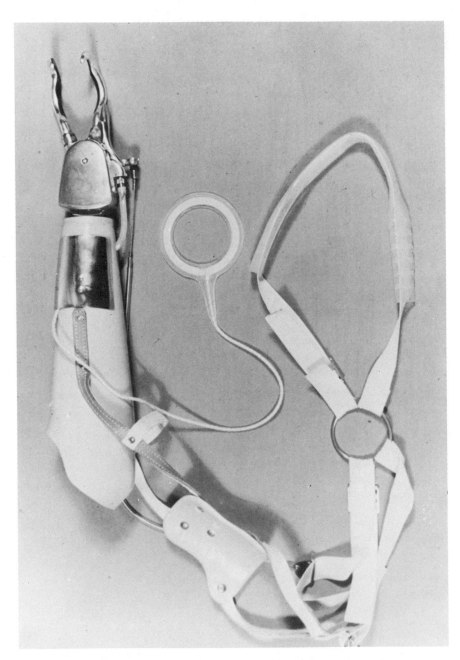

A prosthetic arm devised by Dr. Frank W. Clippinger, Duke University professor of orthopedics, is shown. The amputee wearing this can now even "feel" how hard he is squeezing an object with the prongs.

PART IV

The Prostheses: Artificial Parts of Every Kind

Americans were pleasurably frightened in 1931 by the first bionic man—Boris Karloff who as Frankenstein's legendary monster stomped his way across the silver screen only a very few years after the movies had been converted to sound to become the "talkies." It was in the 1818 book *Frankenstein* by Mary Wollstonecraft Shelley, that this monster first appeared, built entirely out of bits and pieces stolen and salvaged from a variety of human corpses in deserted graveyards. The book became what is probably the most famous pseudoscientific novel of all time, and the movie is one of the most famous and successful ever produced. Like many classics, *Frankenstein* has proven to possess an amazingly realistic core: for only recently have medical scientists learned to salvage tissues and organs from the dead and put them to work in the living, as corneal, kidney, and heart transplants, for example.

But it is the prostheses (the artificial parts) that are most typical of today's bionic people. And these prostheses are many and diverse today. As we will shortly see,

57

fourteen of the world's strongest permanent magnets have been implanted in the jaw of a teenage high-school student to rebuild his face, which was destroyed in an auto accident. Others have had lost noses, ears, fingers, and breasts replaced so that these victims of diseases or accidents could resume normal lives looking like the rest of us once more. Others who have tragically lost limbs have had these replaced with Space Age devices that they can control with their own muscles and nerves much as they once did their natural ones.

Teeth are being replaced with carbon, ceramic, or metal substitute roots implanted into the jaws; tissues are being glued instead of sewed together; and synthetic meshes or steel wires are implanted to repair weakened abdominal tissues. It all adds up to a whole new breed of bionic men and women who benefit greatly from these new artificial additions.

MEDICAL SCULPTING— COSMETIC PROSTHESES

Medical sculpting is a solution for the problems of young and old alike—victims of accidents, diseases, and birth defects. Papers around the world told the tragic story of the teenager who was kidnapped in Italy a few years ago and had his ear cut off to extort a massive ransom from his grandfather, a famous millionaire. Diseases, too, cost people parts of their body. Only recently cancer forced Betty Ford and Happy Rockefeller, the wives of a President and a Vice-President, to have a breast removed. And many children are born with missing or deformed limbs.

Thousands of young and old Americans are affected by these disfiguring absences and losses of body parts every year, and often the psychological scars are worse than the physical ones. Young people especially suffer from the thoughtless ridicule of peers and playmates. So common are such cosmetic problems that a whole new field of medical science has developed to solve them. While doctors prefer to perform reconstructive operations for these losses, this kind of plastic surgery often demands a whole series of operations performed over many months. Moreover, such surgical procedures are usually painful, expensive, and even dangerous for some patients, and even then satisfactory results are not guaranteed.

The man-made prosthetic replacements are technically termed *cosmetic prostheses.* And those who create them are truly medical sculptors. Until a very few years ago, there were less than a dozen such people in our country, but they are now increasing in numbers. These creative artists must approach their reconstructions with the skills of portrait painter, sculptor, and scientific technician. The art and science of medical sculpture dates back at least four hundred years to sixteenth-century Danish astronomer Tycho Brahe, whose observations led to the acceptance of the Copernican theory that the sun, not the earth, was the center of the solar system. However, instead of sticking to his science, Brahe got involved in a duel that cost him his nose, so he promptly made himself a crude nose prosthesis of silver and gold.

We've come a long way since Brahe, and prostheses are now available for many missing body parts. The most common of these, according to the University of Michigan's Mr. Denis C. Lee, professor of medical and biological illustration, and Dr. William R. Harlan, professor of medicine, are those of the ear, nose, eye, finger, and breast. For best results, the materials should match the

defective or missing body part in texture, be strong
and readily formed, and be capable of being tinted to
the desired color. Beside Brahe's metals, the past has
seen the use of ivory, vulcanite, wax, and aluminum for
this purpose. All have now been discarded for the new
synthetic materials and Space Age metals. Silicone rubber is most commonly used because of its natural lifelike
texture, its ease of working and coloring, and its ability to
be hardened without heat.

As Mr. Lee puts it: "I'm the last resort—the place the
Burn Unit and surgeons turn to when they can't recon-
struct a damaged or deformed area." Making a satisfactory cosmetic prosthesis is no simple matter. Placing his
patient in an old dentist's chair in his small examining
room and workshop, Lee first makes an impression of the
damaged area with flexible material. The plaster cast
produced from this impression duplicates the body situa-
tion. This artist then prepares paints to match the color of
the lightest skin adjacent to the missing or damaged
section. For an eye or ear prosthesis, Lee also makes a
cast of the part's mate.

Working from the surviving part or from old photos,
Lee builds a replica of the missing part in clay. He works
directly on the cast so that the replacement will fit the
patient perfectly. A mold is made from this clay replica,
and Lee's special silicone mixture is put into the mold,
where it cures to form the desired restoration. The final
prosthesis is now fitted and trimmed precisely to blend in
with the flesh of the area.

From sculpting Lee now turns to painting, artistically
coloring the prosthesis "just like a portrait" to match the
opposite organ or the surrounding parts. The finished
prosthesis has delicate variations in its tones to make it
virtually indistinguishable from the skin. Lastly, a clear

coating is sprayed on to "lock in" these colors and preserve the naturalness in use. Lee has even developed shading materials the patient himself can apply to make the artificial part match a summer tan or sunburn. Special silicone adhesives hold these devices in place so effectively that the wearer can engage in strenuous activities and even go swimming without fear of dislodging the prosthesis.

The cast is kept on file along with a tinted duplicate. Therefore, if the original prosthesis is damaged or lost, another can be quickly made, colored, and mailed to the patient. On the average, these prostheses last about a year and can be readily and inexpensively duplicated. The prostheses are not affected by extremes of temperatures, but they are best taken off daily for periods of four hours or so to permit the moisture that forms beneath them to evaporate.

Let us now look at some specific prostheses. Probably the easiest part to replace, according to Lee, is the ear, which in coloring and form can usually be matched to the other one. A prosthetic ear is so firmly attached with adhesives that it can readily support eyeglasses or hearing aids. And today's long hair styles are virtually made to order to hide any possible appearance of artificiality.

Probably the most conspicuous is the nose prosthesis, which is often needed to replace an entire organ lost to cancer or injury. However, the natural facial skin folds, shadows, makeup, and today's big tinted eyeglasses all help to hide the presence of a replacement. Hair may even be placed in the nostrils as a filter for foreign material.

Some people may also suffer the loss of an eye and even the whole orbit in which it lies—from surgery for certain eye tumors (retinoblastomas) or accidents. Using an artificial eye as we discussed earlier, the surviving normal eye is first matched, and then the surrounding orbital tissues are replaced with a prosthesis in which eyelashes are embedded for perfection in matching. With the proper safety eyeglasses, the margins of the prosthesis can be hidden.

Typical of the problems Lee deals with are those of a Vietnam veteran who lost an eye and ear in combat. The Michigan medical artist constructed an artificial ear as well as a prosthesis that contained a glass eye and also hid the scar tissue around the damaged eye socket. And for another young person who had lost both eyes to a gun blast, the artist created a lifelike mask for the entire upper face.

As Lee and Dr. Harlan point out, every year thousands of Americans lose hands and feet in whole or in part from a variety of accidents—from industrial machinery (most commonly punch presses), to doors or lawn mowers. When only part of a finger is lost, the prosthesis can be held in place by suction. But when several fingers are lost up to the knuckles or beyond, a "hand" glove may be used. With the zipper hidden in the palm and a wrist-watch or bracelet to hide the wrist end, this looks like the victim's own hand. However, these have to be replaced every six months or so because they become discolored and stained after constant use.

Perhaps the most common of all such prostheses are those needed for the ninety thousand American women that Lee and Harlan estimate undergo radical breast surgery every year. Lee has devised a prosthesis for such women which can be used either with or without a bra. Liquid-filled, it looks, feels, and even moves like the natural remaining organ to which it is matched in every respect.

BIONIC FACES, JAWS, AND TEETH

A talented teenage high-school senior and rock musician recently had his upper jaw totally demolished in a bone-crushing auto accident. This young man had to face the possibility that he would never smile, eat, or speak normally again. Although nearly every bone in the boy's face had been broken, an Albany plastic surgeon stabilized the facial bones and lower jaw. But without the upper jaw, palate, and upper teeth, the face was caved in. Dentists and General Electric magnet experts involved themselves in the problem, and a unique solution was devised.

The GE consultants designed and fashioned fourteen pill-sized supermagnets. Half the size of an aspirin tablet, each was so powerful that a 2-ounce magnet could carry a 350-pound weight. A two-piece, 3-ounce methylmethacrylate resin prosthesis was built to replace the entire missing palate and upper jaw into which ten magnets were strategically embedded. Finally, a full denture to replace the missing upper teeth was constructed, and four more magnets were embedded there. The denture clicks into position, and now this young musician's face no longer reveals the evidence of his massive injury: a unique achievement for those who deal with such accidents.

Dental implants are being increasingly tried with a wide variety of materials and methods. The materials used have already been discussed; they are buried in the jaw bones as frames or pins or screws. These have posts protruding through the gums to serve as the base on which bridges or single caps are placed. Carbon, ceramic, or methylmethacrylate roots are also buried in the jaw bones, and teeth are built on these "roots."

METALS, PLASTICS, AND GLUES FOR BIONIC PEOPLE

A hernia is a protrusion of any organ or tissue from its normal cavity. But the word "hernia" usually refers to the condition in which a weak spot in the abdominal cavity wall permits intestine to press through either regularly or occasionally. So common is this problem that hernia operations to repair this weakness are by far the most frequent of all operations. Surgeons today may use Marlex—polypropylene, a synthetic fabric—mesh to reinforce their repair and prevent a recurrence of this problem. Some experts even use metal sutures to provide added strength to their repairs.

And then there are tissue glues, real Space Age stuff whose very discovery is intriguing. A scientist doing experiment number ten on page nine of his laboratory notebook put a drop of colorless liquid between two prisms to see how it affected light rays. Much to his surprise, he later found he couldn't separate the prisms or dissolve the material no matter how hard he tried. Eastman Kodak named the liquid (from the experiment and page) Eastman 910 adhesive, and it proved to be one of a whole family of superglues, chemicals called cyanoacrylates.

One widespread story is that a scientist got a drop on his finger and scratched his ear—before he'd finished scratching, his finger was stuck to his ear and had to be separated surgically. Did this really happen? No one is sure. But it is typical of these cyanoacrylates, which stick wet or dry tissues together, and this has been their use in the field of bionics. In fact, these glues are so powerful that a drop of the thin clear liquid produces a bond strong enough to lift an automobile with four people in it!

64

The newer cyanoacrylates have proven self-sterilizing and able to control bleeding. Surgeons using them must wear polyethylene gloves over their conventional rubber ones to prevent the gloves from sticking to everything they touch. These superglues saved the lives of many soldiers in the Vietnam war by controlling abdominal bleeding from severe wounds. They have also been used by ophthalmologists to seal corneal perforations, to glue on contact prostheses, and even to attach radioactive plaques to the eyeball for the treatment of eye tumors. The role of the cyanoacrylates in bionic people is intriguing but still not fully explored or known. More fully developed is . . .

THE NEW WORLD OF BIONIC LIMBS

We've come a long way since Long John Silver in *Treasure Island* stomped about on his peg leg, or Captain Hook in *Peter Pan* used his terrible hook on his enemies. Increasingly, today's Space Age techniques of electronics and sophisticated engineering are being used to help those who have lost all or part of their limbs. Where limb stumps are retained after amputation or accident, it is now possible for these people to actually "feel" what they do with their new prosthetic limbs, to control these prostheses much as they once did with their own natural limbs.

When you tense a muscle, it generates an electrical current of a few thousandths of a volt: the stronger the tension, the greater the voltage. Dr. Robert W. Mann, a Massachusetts Institute of Technology professor of biomedical engineering, has turned this knowledge into the pioneering "Boston arm." With a complex prosthesis restoring an arm amputated above the elbow, Mann has used an electrical receiver taped to the muscles of the arm stump to pick up these tiny electrical (EMG) signals. When amplified, these EMG signals can be used to operate a small motor that moves the prosthetic arm up and down. The harder the muscles contract, the greater the EMG voltage and the faster the arm moves. The heavier the weight grasped by the prosthesis with its two-pronged hook or "hand," the greater is the EMG signal and muscle effort needed. The amputee can thus judge, or "feel," that the weight is heavier, just as we do with our own natural arms when we lift a package or bag.

The usual and most effective prosthetic hand is a two-pronged hook that closes on an object—book, telephone, cup, whatever—to lift or move or use it. Dr. Frank W. Clippinger, a Duke University professor of orthopedics, has devised an artificial arm that goes a step further. He has implanted a radio receiver in the arm stump against its nerve. On the skin over this receiver is an antenna connected to a gauge in the hook; this gauge transmits a signal to the arm stump nerve telling the amount of pressure exerted by the prongs of the hook on objects. Thus, the amputee now "feels" how hard he is squeezing. More like a natural hand than ever before, this Clippinger artificial arm permits its owner to pick up delicate objects without danger of crushing them in a Frankenstein-like grip, unknowing and unfeeling of the pressure exerted.

It's all a far cry from Captain Hook and Long John Silver. Dr. Mann is working on a similar approach to artificial knees so that the peg leg will finally advance to an electronic prosthesis, which will be as controllable by its owner as today's electronic arms. Such devices are proving invaluable as they make life more practical and much more normal for the many amputees in our society. A variety of electronic prosthetic arms are now actually

available, and new ones are being introduced all the
time. While a similar electronic leg is still in the experimental stage, it, too, will eventually make it possible for
leg amputees to enjoy something far closer to the normal
walking we all enjoy than the mechanical prostheses
conventionally available.

PART V

Bionic Bones, Joints, and Muscles

Frankenstein's monster clanked around on the silver screen, no doubt because his muscles and joints were stiff, ailing, or troubled. Many people, young and old, suffer these same problems, but now there are ways of treating them, or replacing the defective joints with ones that function smoothly and painlessly. There are even man-made muscles and bones. All the body joints—fingers and toes; wrists, elbows, and shoulders; hips, ankles, and knees—are being replaced with artificial ones in increasing numbers today. The National Bureau of Standards estimates that "in the United States alone, more than one million individual orthopedic implants are surgically inserted each year, ranging from metal nails and screws to plates, pins, and prostheses."

It was not long after Mary Shelley wrote *Frankenstein* that doctors began their assault on body joints (about the same time corneas were first being replaced). In 1827 a Philadelphia surgeon, Dr. John Rhea Barton, carried out the first operation on the hips. He operated to remedy an arthritic condition that had made the joint rigid. But it was 1891 before surgeons began to insert prostheses into the hip joints.

The first total hip prosthesis was inserted by a Romanian surgeon and professor in Berlin, Dr. T. Gluck. Since that first daring operation on the hip at the very end of the last century, much progress has been made. Today all arm and leg joints can be replaced, and every year American orthopedic surgeons insert nearly a hundred thousand artificial hips alone. This surgery has changed from a rare and daring operation to a virtually routine surgical procedure. Almost invariably successful, it is performed on patients from pre-teens to those in their 90s.

It was the hip whose replacement heralded the era of artificial joints and whose surgery is the most fully and successfully developed. We can best explore joint implants by looking at this one in detail as a prototype for the others.

NEW HIPS FOR OLD

The hip joint is essentially a ball-and-socket joint, the type used in mechanical devices to attain maximum range of motion in every direction. This vast degree of freedom for the leg is needed for you to walk and kick, climb mountains or stairs, run, sit, or squat, etc. To make these motions all possible, nature made the hip joint so that the head of the femur, the thigh bone, fits into a cone or socket in the hip or pelvic bone.

T. Gluck's first artificial hip employed surprisingly advanced materials and concepts. An ivory billiard ball is very similar to the head of the femur: it is perfectly round and very dense and smooth to reduce friction in movement. Obtained from the tusk or upper front tooth of the elephant, ivory is a bonelike tissue and produces minimal tissue reaction. To cement this to the femur Gluck used a combination of rosin and plaster of paris, both relatively compatible materials. In fact, the use of an ivory ball here was to continue for some forty years.

It wasn't until the very early 1930s that new ideas brought a whole improved world of artificial joints. Boston surgeon Dr. Marius Nygaard Smith-Petersen tried out a wide range of materials, including pyrex, and even the few plastics of the day. At this time, others were trying out different materials including zinc, silver, and magnesium. But in the 1930s, too, came those materials which more than any others have opened the way to the reality of the Six Million Dollar Man's joints: vitallium (a cobalt-chromium alloy) and methylmethacrylate were introduced for dentures and proved to have outstanding characteristics for implants of all kinds.

Then a British orthopedic surgeon, Dr. G. K. McKee, attempted a total hip prosthesis, one in which both the head of the femur and the hip socket were replaced with artificial materials. Dr. McKee's attempt proved unsuccessful, but in 1942 a South Carolina medical journal carried the first report of a successful metal hip prosthesis. It wasn't until the late 1950s, however, that Dr. John Charnley, a professor of orthopedics at England's University of Manchester, opened this new surgical era with his total hip replacements. His new prosthesis used stainless steel for the ball and framework, and polyethylene for the hip socket.

Charnley's work was so successful that the technique spread widely on both sides of the Atlantic. He came to the United States in 1974 to receive our coveted Lasker Research Award for this work. He was even photographed with a ballerina who had had her own right hip replaced just a year earlier. She was already able to perform a pirouette for the photographers while pro-claiming to the world, "It's just miraculous!" By that time, Charnley and his surgical team had already carried out some ten thousand total hip replacements with a failure rate of only 1 or 2 percent. And a 1976 survey on our own side of the Atlantic found surgeons inserting nearly a hundred thousand total hip prostheses every year. The era of the bionic people was in full swing and was taken for granted by the medical profession and public alike. Artificial hips and a flock of other replacements are considered routine surgery today and are not even remarked upon by anyone.

Arthritis sufferers are the most frequent candidates for hip joint replacements, but these prostheses also benefit victims of accidents or tumors. The arthritis may be either the rheumatoid kind, which can begin in infancy, or osteoarthritis, which is either the result of years of wear and tear or the effect of abuse, excessive use, or injuries. Osteoarthritis can occur in the young if the joint is subjected to the kind of stress knees are subjected to in football or basketball. Artificial hip joints must be extremely strong, for even ordinary walking throws on them a pressure equal to three times the actual weight of the person. These prostheses are increasingly used for the young, so they must be able to bear the burdens of a half century or more of use.

The artificial hip joint itself must be friction-free so that no lubrication is needed for the virtually constant movement that goes on in this joint. Moreover, the joint must be designed so that activity and pressure won't dislodge it. Finally, the prosthesis must have enough elasticity to absorb some of the shock produced by heels hitting the pavements in walking or running—which is why plastics are used for these sockets.

The hip-replacement surgery takes only a few hours. The head of the natural femur is removed and a seat is prepared for a new socket in the hip bone. The ball is cemented into the femur and the socket part into the hip bone. The cement is methylmethacrylate (liquid and powder are mixed together to form a sticky dough), which sets quickly. By the end of a week or so the newly bionic person is up and walking around on a new hip.

A wide range of materials is used for these hip implants. Charnley's own device had a stainless steel head with a long shaft that was cemented into the thigh bone with methylmethacrylate, which was also used to cement the plastic socket into a prepared seat in the hip bone. The Russians have introduced an all-aluminum hip prosthesis, in which ball and socket do not come apart; no cement is required because the metal locks into the bone.

Regardless of the type of prosthesis used, the success runs over 95 percent, as shown by studies checking on the resulting freedom from substantial pain, ability to walk and use the hip, and improvement over the original difficulties.

THE OTHER ARTIFICIAL ARM AND LEG JOINTS

Fingers and toes, elbows and shoulders, knees and ankles, all are being replaced today. None, however, is yet at the level of development of the hip replacements because the other joints are more complex and present special problems. Farthest advanced are the artificial knees.

The knee joint is a complex one with a considerable range of motion. Notice the ways your knee must move when you use your lower leg in various ways and positions—walking, running, climbing, dancing, and engaging in different sports. In everyday activities you put five times your entire body weight on this joint. And the athletes who rebound on them in basketball or get hit on them in football or pound them in track-and-field events must absorb much more stress. Not surprisingly, these joints do break down from such excessive demands as well as from accidents and arthritis.

The knee joint prosthesis has changed greatly since one of the first—a simple metal hinge—was introduced in the early 1950s by Sweden's Dr. Borje Walldius. This device is still being improved upon today. One of the latest versions is a complex affair with a combination of metal riding on plastic and a metal ball fitting into a plastic socket. This device attempts to imitate and restore the natural joint motions and prevent dislocation.

A 1976 survey indicates that thirty thousand total knee replacements were installed that year, compared to eighty thousand total hips. Experts agree that while great progress has been made, there is much to be done before the total knees catch up with the total hips. So today's bionic people can't do as well with their knees as with their hips and are likely to have even less success replacing the other joints in their arms and legs.

Meanwhile a 23-year-old mailman is believed to be the first person in the United States to have had artificial ankle joints inserted in both legs. Orthopedic surgeons at Brooklyn's Downstate Medical Center, finding both of the patient's ankle joints destroyed, cemented plastic blocks with concave surfaces to the end of the large bones of the lower leg, and convex metal devices to the foot to fit into the concave plastic blocks. Dr. Eduardo Alvarez, the professor of orthopedic surgery who performed the operation, feels that such artificial ankle replacements are still experimental and the few attempted are too recent for adequate follow-up evaluation.

The joints of the feet and toes are some of the most commonly stricken in rheumatoid arthritis. More than 90 percent of those who suffer with this disease for any length of time develop foot problems. Doctors are currently using silicone rubber implants to replace these joints. Similar ones are being used for the fingers of the hand: these are simply one-piece hinges of silicone rubber. In 1970 Dr. Alfred B. Swanson of Grand Rapids, Michigan, an orthopedic surgeon and leading developer of these implants, found that such hinges could be flexed at least 100 million times without breaking. And it's now reported that a similar finger joint of flexible synthetic rubber has stood up to 300 million flexes without failing.

The shoulder joint, too, presents problems. When you lift something in your hand, the weight pivots on your shoulder with enormous stress. Although some dozen different shoulder implants have been developed, the total shoulder replacement is still not as developed as either the hip or knee. Yet a surgical team headed by Dr. Melvin Post, chairman of orthopedics at Chicago's famous Michael Reese Hospital and Medical Center, has developed a ball-and-socket type metal and plastic shoulder joint that has successfully survived an almost incredible amount of abuse in patients from their mid-20s to late 70s.

The Chicago team finds its patients have used this joint for such sports as lacrosse and racquetball, mountain climbing, and weightlifting, and have even been able to withstand a rifle recoil in deer hunting. These shoulder implants have survived accidents severe enough to fracture other bones. The team reports nine of their shoulder-implant patients experienced thirty major accidents: some of the implants survived these injuries, and those that did fail were successfully replaced. The team sums it up: "Pain relief was dramatic. . . . More than 90% reported much less pain after the implant operations."

Elbow prostheses are not even as far along as those for the shoulder. The elbow must twist, rotate, and bend in an incredibly fluid series of movements. Doctors have tried a variety of replacement devices, including all-silicone and silicone-metal implants. But a new one devised by Dr. Frederick C. Ewald, orthopedic surgeon of Boston's Robert B. Brigham Hospital, has a curved metal hinge riding in a plastic block, which restores most of the elbow's range of motion. Describing this still-experimental joint, Dr. Clement B. Sledge, Brigham's famous surgeon in chief, recently said: "Thus far it has proven itself to be a very effective means of relieving pain and increasing function in the rheumatoid elbow."

Newest and most experimental of all is the artificial wrist. With the many small hand bones involved and a diverse and complex range of motions, the problem here is unique. The different metal and plastic implants have rods that are cemented into as many as three or four different arm and hand bones. The prosthesis itself is essentially a ball-and-socket device, although it may move on more than one axis. Although experience with it is limited, the wrist replacement does provide relief of pain, but with some limitation of normal movement. While the outlook is hopeful, the wrist joint is clearly in an early stage of development with many changes to come.

ARTIFICIAL BONES, MUSCLES, AND SPINES

Bone replacement is reminiscent of Frankenstein as well as the plastic or bionic person, for doctors now use cadaver bones as substitutes for those they must remove because of cancer. In the United States as well as in France and the Soviet Union, surgeons now remove a section of bone from a cadaver and deep-freeze it at -30° C. Just before use, they tailor this to fit the recipient's missing bone. The cadaver bone is then fixed in place with metal pins or screws, and the recipient's muscles and ligaments are attached. This has virtually always proven a successful and functional replacement. So Mary Shelley was looking ahead some century and a half when she wrote her book!

Medical science is having much success dealing with otosclerosis, a disease in which the tiny bones in the middle ear become fixed and are no longer able to vibrate and transmit sound. An operation is now performed to free these bones so that they can again both vibrate and transmit sound. One or the other of these bones may be replaced with a variety of implants—stainless steel or tantalum wires, silastic, or Teflon.

A Japanese orthopedic surgeon has used titanium and polyethylene to fashion and insert an entire thigh bone, the femur, after the patient's own had to be removed because of cancer. Along with this he included total hip and knee joints. And no one can possibly know how many millions of pins, nails, and supporting metal plates have been installed in people with broken bones—among them teenage football players who then go right back to the gridiron!

Spines, too, are getting a variety of metal and plastic materials attached and inserted. The replacement here is a kind of reinforced concrete bridge across the section of spine that is weak or broken. A stainless steel mesh placed across the damaged bone area is filled with methylmethacrylate cement, and the resulting permanent support makes it possible for the injured to walk again, with crutches perhaps, but to walk when otherwise they would be using wheelchairs the rest of their lives. And a Polish orthopedic surgeon has used paired coil springs inserted onto each side of the spinal column to stabilize fractured spines while the broken vertebra knits.

Devised in Australia, and now in use here, is a method of cable stitching the spine to correct severe spinal curvature deformities in children. Using metal screws, staples, and a cable, the orthopedic surgeon applies pressure to straighten the spine and keep it that way. This method is only used in certain very extreme cases, where the curvature is producing a whole range of nerve and other problems threatening eventual crippling.

Meanwhile, at the Battelle Memorial Institute in Columbus, Ohio, a team of scientists headed by Dr. David L. Gardner is working on a prosthetic device that may do the job of muscles that cannot function. Dr. Gardner describes his artificial muscle as a passive device that works like a rubber band. If a person, for example, could straighten his or her arm but not bend it back, the built-in tension of the artificial muscle could bring the arm back to its bent position.

Gardner's artificial muscles are still limited to experimental use in animals, but the scientist believes they may be used in humans in the foreseeable future. Meanwhile, there are nearly a million people in the United States alone suffering from muscular dystrophy, strokes, cerebral palsy, muscular atrophy, and other conditions that might be helped by such an implantable muscle.

The actual device is a silicone tube surrounding another tube of Dacron fabric (a little like your jacket's sleeve over your shirtsleeve). The Dacron serves as an artificial tendon and protrudes from both ends of the silicone tube for attachment either to a natural tendon or directly to the bone. Inside the wider central portion of this "muscle," the fabric is pleated and bunched together to provide freedom of movement. Just as natural muscle stretches only so far, the extension of the artificial muscle is limited by the amount of fabric used.

Implanted under tension to replace one muscle of an antagonistic pair, the elastic prosthesis simply counterbalances the normal tension, or "tone," of the opposing muscle. When it is stretched by the opposing muscle, it stores energy; as the natural muscle relaxes, this energy itself brings the limb back to its resting position. It's all been tried successfully, but only in sheep legs. If it works in one animal, however, there is no reason it shouldn't work in another, and that other might be the human being.

PART VI

New Organs for Bionic People—Implants and Transplants

We've already talked of many things for the bionic person of bones, muscles, and joints; sight and hearing; pain-control devices; and much more. The value of all this is incontestable, but man can survive without the use of most bones, muscles, and joints, without sight or hearing. There are other parts, however, without whose proper functioning he cannot live, his heart and kidneys, for example. Their replacements make up most of this chapter. Here, too, we will talk of something that neither the bionic or plastic person nor even Frankenstein's monster has: transplants of living organs—the perfect replacements for hopelessly damaged, failing, or defective ones.

Right now more than sixty thousand people across the world are being kept alive by artificial organs. And some twenty thousand are living on organs donated by relatives or obtained from the cadavers of strangers. These organs carry out the job of their natural ones, which for one reason or another have failed. Neither age nor sex are barriers, and the beneficiaries of these artificial and natural replacements range in age from 6 weeks to 83 years. The great success in both artificial organs and transplanted ones has come with the kidney first and predominately; the heart ranks a dramatic second with growing promise. So let us look at these in detail.

THE KIDNEYS

Your kidneys are twin bean-shaped little organs, each the size of your fist, buried in your back below your ribs. They are not very impressive to look at, yet your life depends on these two organs. Should they both fail, you would soon die—at least that's how it used to be. Now, however, there are artificial kidneys and miracle transplants to restore you to a virtually normal life. The kidney is so essential to life that nature has provided a sort of fail-safe system in the form of a vast excess of capacity. You have two kidneys when you can easily and safely get along perfectly well on one. Their functioning capacity is so great that these organs could process nine times as much fluid as they actually handle; and if 90 percent of their functioning tissue was destroyed or suddenly failed, these organs could still go on working well enough so that with proper medical management you might yet have a long life.

The kidneys are the master chemists of your body, precision chemical factories and filtration units. They process more than 18 gallons of blood every hour to remove excess fluid and chemicals as well as cleanse the blood of waste products. These twin organs must function with absolute precision: if just a whisper too much of any one chemical (even ordinary table salt) is allowed to remain in the blood, disaster can result. Too much salt in the blood causes legs, hands, face, and body to puff up like a balloon, eventually causing heart failure; too much potassium can stop the heart like a shot, while too little can paralyze the breathing muscles. If the kidneys cease to function, the body swells, poisonous waste products accumulate in the blood, and coma and death invariably follow.

There are a considerable number of kidney diseases. In the United States alone, nearly 10 million suffer from these problems, while nearly another 4 million have unrecognized or undiagnosed disorders. There are kidney diseases that strike in the first weeks and months of life and others which can strike at any age. Every year, in fact, some sixty thousand Americans die of kidney disease, and the numbers in other countries are comparable.

It was long obvious to doctors that if patients afflicted with kidney disease were to be saved, some way must be found to cleanse their blood of impurities and poisons. During World War II, Willem Kolff was a young Dutch physician. Deeply disturbed by a young patient who had died of kidney disease, Dr. Kolff began work on an artificial kidney. In this method known as dialysis, the blood passes through cellophane tubing outside the body: accumulated impurities are removed by the solution through which these tubes carry their precious liquid before returning it to the body. Working in secret with clandestine materials and equipment while Nazi soldiers tramped overhead, Kolff built his dialysis machine, the first artificial kidney. He had to use wooden staves instead of metal frames for the revolving drums, and sausage skins provided the cellophane. He treated the first patient suffering with fatal kidney disease with his artificial kidney on March 17, 1943, but the patient died. The first life Dr. Kolff saved with the artificial kidney was his seventeenth patient. This great success occurred on September 11, 1945. Dr. Kolff's achievement not only opened the door to a new world of artificial organs but also contributed to our current success with the kidney transplant program.

Since Dr. Kolff's early work, little more than thirty years ago, devices and techniques have improved greatly. Today patients can live with an artificial kidney for many years. The device is too new to permit doctors to estimate how long a patient can continue to use it, but some already have used it for a dozen years. It's helped people of all ages and lifestyles, making it possible for a young attorney to continue his practice, a housewife to travel in Europe for nearly three weeks, a student to graduate from medical school with honors, and many young women to bear healthy, normal children.

Those whose kidneys have failed usually need two to three weekly treatments of four to eight hours each on the artificial kidney, during which time the person is connected by tubes to a large stationary device the size of a washing machine. The patients are immobilized while their blood is passed through the device and cleansed of its impurities before being returned to the body. Dr. Kolff is now working on a portable artificial kidney with which a person, as he puts it, "can go to the door to let in the dog or the mailman, or welcome the children when they come home." Wearers can go for a walk for about fifteen minutes with this device, then return to a tank slightly larger than an electric typewriter to refresh the device for another fifteen minutes. Ideally, such a person would only be dialyzed two hours a day, anywhere. This tank could fit under the seat of a plane or be buckled into the adjoining car seat, and it's so quiet it could even be worn to the movies. Even more desirable, of course, is to replace failed kidneys with natural ones—kidney transplants. And here the success can only be described as phenomenal.

In Oklahoma lives a seemingly typical housewife, the mother of several children. But actually she is a biological rarity—an identical twin. Only once in roughly three hundred births does her kind occur. Unlike fraternal twins, identical twins are so perfectly matched that they are more like the right and left sides of the same person than two different ones. They have as many as thirty blood group tests that are the same, and their fingerprints are similar. And, most important of all, you can graft a piece of skin from one to the other and it will grow without rejection.

When this woman's kidneys failed in 1956, her identical twin donated one kidney. It was transplanted by a medical and surgical team headed by Dr. John P. Merrill of Boston's Peter Bent Brigham Hospital. This was then a daring operation, for only one other such procedure had ever been successful. The woman has since had two children, and the donated kidney is still working as well as ever—the oldest organ transplant in history!

Things have come a long way since the 1950s. In the first nine years of our transplant era there were only 123 kidney transplants. The numbers increased, and in 1962 there were sixty-seven transplants, and these were more than doubled in 1963 and again in 1964. In 1968 there were over a thousand kidney transplants and more than seventeen hundred in 1971. And these operations have continued to increase. Today they are being performed at a rate of more than two thousand a year. A 6-week-old recipient has been given a kidney from a 6-year-old.

When the transplanted kidney comes from an identical twin, the success rate is currently well over 90 percent and failures are usually the result of technical slip-ups, such as surgical accidents. When the donors are living relatives, these transplants are about 80 percent successful for one or two years and those kidneys that survive this long seem to have permanent success. Brother or sister donor kidneys are some 5 to 10 percent more successful than parental ones. Cadaver kidneys have been 40 to 50 percent successful over the first two-year period, but there is some indication that this rate may be improving. On January 1, 1975, the Organ Transplant Registry, which was then receiving most worldwide data on transplants, reported that some twenty thousand kidneys had been transplanted and eight thousand of these were functional.

Actually, it was the artificial kidney that made possible the success of transplantation, along with the fact that we all have two kidneys when we need only one. Patients with an identical twin willing and able to donate a kidney are ideally situated, those with such fraternal twins somewhat less so. Even those with willing sisters or brothers or parents still have reason to be optimistic should a kidney fail.

But many whose kidneys fail must turn to cadaver kidneys, and this means waiting for the right match to come along. Thanks to the artificial kidney, which can serve in the interim, such waiting is safe today even if it takes months or years. Then, too, there are those whose transplanted kidney also fails. But, again, the artificial kidney assures continued life; later a second transplant can be tried, and these often succeed. While the outlook for those whose kidneys fail today is a bright one, the same cannot be said for another organ whose failure is much more common and whose replacement must lie chiefly in the bionic area . . .

THE HEART

The very word "heart" evokes a feeling of mysticism, importance, and an ultimate essentialness for life. Yet Houston's Dr. Denton A. Cooley, world-famous pioneering heart surgeon and the first to implant a total mechanical heart into a human being, explained that the heart is "one of the simpler visceral organs (the soft organs in chest and abdomen) in this regard: most other organs serve a dual or triple or even quadruple purpose, but the heart is only a pump."

In this simplicity of function lies the way for the heart's successful replacement. However, there is a problem with hearts that does not exist with kidneys: you can't donate your heart to someone and continue to live. Moreover, cadaver hearts are often aged or diseased, and only relatively young, healthy ones can be used for transplants. These are available chiefly as the result of accidental deaths in young people.

Dr. Kolff, also one of the leaders in the development of an artificial heart, points out: "With six hundred thousand people dying (in the United States) from simple coronary heart infarcts (heart attacks) and forty-five thousand being killed by automobiles in the same time period, you will never be able to close the gap between need and availability of hearts for transplantation . . . the use of animal organs is very unlikely since the survival time of these tissues in the normal animal is so short. *Therefore,* we should concentrate on artificial hearts." And, as Dr. Cooley has maintained, the heart's function is so simple that all we really need here is a properly designed and adequately powered pump.

But let us see how the normal heart does function. Your heart is essentially a muscle about the size of a fist, some

5 inches long and 3½ inches wide in the adult. It acts as a four-chambered pressure pump. Blood from the veins enters the two upper chambers (the atria), and passes through valves into the lower chambers (the larger and more heavily muscled ventricles). It then goes through another set of valves into the pulmonary artery (the one to the lungs) and the aorta, the chief artery of the body from which all the other arteries spring as they divide and subdivide to carry blood throughout your body. In a seventy-year life span your heart will beat some 3 billion times and pump about half a million tons of blood. When the ventricles fill with blood and contract to pump it out, the pressure of the blood slams the valves between atria and ventricles shut, so that no blood seeps back and pressure is maintained for the circulation through the body. The valves between ventricles and outgoing arteries also shut the same way for the same reason. Defective valves can cause trouble through inadequate circulation; these can often be detected by the distinctive sounds (heart murmurs) they make.

In December 1967 the world was startled and thrilled to hear that South Africa's Dr. Christiaan Barnard had performed the world's first heart transplant operation at Capetown. The recipient was Philip Blaiberg, and his nineteen-month survival stirred the world's hopes. Such transplants reached a high of twenty-six in November 1968, but the many failures due to rejection or the infections resulting from the drugs used to suppress the immune reaction soon discouraged doctors and patients alike. By the early 1970s, hearts were being transplanted only once or twice a month.

By the end of the first decade of heart transplantation—December 1977—at least 354 heart transplants had been performed in the world but only eighty-five of the recipients were still alive. A Frenchman was in his tenth year and had even outlived his own surgeon, and another recipient, who had received his heart at Stanford University in California, was in his eighth year.

It's not the surgery that's the problem but the rejection. Fighting rejection with immunosuppressive drugs unfortunately exposes the patient to infection, as we discussed in Part I. The operation itself is like preparing a pumpkin for Halloween. The bottom three-quarters of the recipient heart is removed, leaving the stem (a goodly portion of the atria) with all its vein connections intact. The new bottom part is simply sewn on and connected to the pulmonary artery and aorta.

In April 1969 Dr. Cooley, as a last desperate measure, implanted a mechanical heart into a man whom it kept alive for the two and a half days of frantic searching it took to find a heart for transplantation. Although the patient died two days after this surgery anyhow, it did prove the possibilities of an artificial heart. Work on such devices has continued with growing hope. Many animals have survived with mechanical hearts: the longevity record is held by Abebe, a Holstein calf that lived with an air-powered device for 184 days. By the time you read this, there will probably be a better record, as these improve almost every day.

Artificial hearts are driven by external compressed-air power units (like the one Cooley implanted) or by electric motors. Atomic energy has also been suggested as a power source. According to Dr. Kolff: "As much plutonium-238 as is in a small salt shaker gives off 33 watts of power and that is enough to drive an artificial heart." In fact, this element is so powerful that there has even been concern expressed that such patients might be kidnapped by terrorists to secure the plutonium in their hearts as a weapon.

Obviously, the way of the future is going to be the artificial heart, and success in this area is likely to come about in the foreseeable future. In fact, in December 1977 the Associated Press reported that an international team of surgeons in Zurich, Switzerland, had successfully used a total artificial heart for two days. Used externally and connected by tubes to the patient's own heart, the device acted as a blood pump until the natural heart could start functioning normally again. The device is said to have been used on two other people as well.

Partial artificial hearts, so-called assistance devices intended for use from a few hours right up to permanent implantation, have been used experimentally. On a handful of patients not expected to survive, a left ventricular assistance device has been tried. This adds pumping power to the blood coming from the left ventricle and drives it through the body's vascular system when the heart is no longer able to do the job by itself.

The intra-aortic balloon pump is an accepted and widely used device. When a massive heart attack threatens the life of the victim, a small cut is made in the femoral artery in the thigh. A 10-inch-long cigar-shaped balloon attached to a long tube is then slipped through the arterial system until it reaches the aorta close to the heart. It's said to have been used already in more than ten thousand patients worldwide, and a recent study at Massachusetts General Hospital showed that survival rates nearly tripled with its use.

The balloon collapses as the heart pumps blood into the aorta. The balloon is then filled with gentle pulses of helium from an external machine. These pulsations give the blood an extra push by filling the aorta and squeezing the blood along. This helps the heart to rest so that it can recover to the point where it is once more able to take on its full load in driving the blood throughout the arterial system.

Meanwhile, the insertion of artificial heart valves for those that are defective either as a result of disease or malformation has become a very routine kind of surgery since their introduction in 1958. These devices come in a broad range of designs and materials. They may be simple ball-type valves in which a tiny cage permits the ball to move out of position and allows the blood to flow through, then sets and seals the opening so no blood can seep back through the valve. There are other valves formed of leaflets or tilting disks that do the same thing with wings or flat plates. Materials used run the gamut of those metals and plastics already discussed.

Sections of blood vessels that develop weaknesses are also repaired today with patches of various synthetic fabrics. Sometimes whole sections of vessels are replaced so that the bionic person may even have artificial blood vessels.

THE OTHER REPLACEABLE ORGANS

Hundreds of times every day in the United States patients who undergo open-heart surgery have an artificial heart and lung pumping and oxygenating their blood. While surgery is going on, these patients are truly bionic people. Now doctors are dreaming of an artificial lung that will take over breathing for as long as three weeks: a potential lifeline for the half million Americans who each year develop temporary or life-threatening lung failure. Lung transplants have not been very successful and are now considered only a last resort.

Dr. J. Donald Hill of San Francisco's Pacific Medical Center sees hope not only for these temporary lung-failure victims but as he explains: "The final step in artificial lung development will be the permanent implantable lung for those patients who have chronically debilitating lung disease which prevents . . . normal life and eventually causes their death." As he sums up lung transplants: ". . . the problems of availability and rejection are almost as difficult to overcome as developing the artificial lung."

An exciting hope for America's 5 million diabetics also lies in an artificial organ. Diabetes is caused by a disturbance of the pancreas in which its tissue (called the islets of Langerhans) fails to produce insulin to control the body's blood sugar. A number of teams have been working on a device that will automatically monitor the blood sugar and dispense insulin or sugar directly into the bloodstream as the body needs it. This artificial pancreas duplicates the natural organ's own functioning, delivering the insulin as needed round the clock. It's a vast improvement over our current method, in which diabetics must give themselves insulin injections at arbitrary times and in fixed amounts. This artificial pancreas has already been used, but the device is so large that it cannot possibly be implanted. That is the aim for the future.

Work toward pancreas transplants is also progressing. A leading concept involves implanting islets in a sealed plastic bag with microscopic holes in its walls. The holes would be of a size to permit insulin and nutrients to pass through but hold back the white blood cells and lymphocytes, which could initiate the mechanism of rejection and destroy the transplanted tissue.

Then there is even implantation of a so-called artificial

gut, known as hyperalimentation. There are, in fact, more than a hundred Americans today who have had large portions of their intestines removed (commonly for cancer) and so need feeding directly through their veins. These people receive medically formulated combinations of liquid nutrients—sugar, fats, proteins, minerals, and vitamins—which are poured into a specially constructed vest they wear along with a lightweight pump and a small battery. This "food" is pumped into the bloodstream to nourish these people. The batteries are plugged into the house current for recharging at night; and while they sleep, these people continue "eating."

The oldest person with a successful artificial gut was 64 years of age, and the youngest was a 21-month-old infant who suffers from a very rare metabolic disorder and must receive special nutrients to survive.

There are other artificial parts that also smack of the plastic person and involve the digestive system as well. There are people who for various reasons (commonly cancer but also injuries of various kinds) find their esophagus or gullet unusable because it has become impassable or has actually been removed. There is now an artificial esophagus for people who previously have had no way to swallow their food. It has been used both here and in Japan, where it was developed. External tubes are installed: attached to the throat at the base of the neck, these tubes run down to a point below the ribs, where they reenter the body to end in the stomach. When these people are not eating, they can remove the tubes to prevent skin irritation.

And now there is also help available for those sufferers who for various reasons have lost the ability to control the ring-like sphincter muscles, which close off the urinary bladder's opening and so make urination impossible. This problem afflicts all paraplegics, and anyone who suffers a spinal cord injury.

This implanted artificial sphincter consists of a cuff, which circles the urethra (the tube leading from the bladder to the outside). This collar is inflated or deflated by bulbs that pump fluid from a reservoir into or out of the cuff, thus closing off the urethra or leaving it free for the urine to pass out. The bulbs are implanted just under the skin, so they can be operated by hand. Urination is thus voluntarily controlled. This device, implanted by a University of Michigan surgical team, has been used for individuals ranging in age from 12 years to 78. And a French surgeon has even implanted an artificial ureter, the tube from the kidneys to the urinary bladder, using silicone and polyester fabrics.

One can only look to the future with hope for a life in which many of the health problems that currently torment human beings will be resolved in ways we may not even fully envision today. And we can recall Dr. Kolff's summary of the future applications of artificial organs: "There is no limit to what technology can accomplish!"

Select Bibliography and Reading List

Adolph, E.F. "The Heart's Pacemaker." *Scientific American,* March 1967.

Deaton, J.G. *New Parts For Old.* Palisade, New Jersey: Franklin Publishing Co., 1974.

Dobelle, W.H. "Current Status of Research on Providing Sight to the Blind." *Journal of Visual Impairment and Blindness,* September 1977.

Freese, A.S. *The Miracle of Vision.* New York: Harper & Row, 1977.

Glabman, S., and Freese, A.S. *Your Kidneys. . . .* New York: E.P. Dutton, 1976.

Jacobs, M. "A New Lease on an Active Life Through Surgical Implants." *Dimensions,* August 1976.

Kolff, W.J. *Artificial Organs.* New York: Halsted Press, 1976.

Laing, P.G. "Tissue Reaction to Biomaterials." *Retrieval and Analysis of Orthopaedic Implants,* National Bureau of Standards, 1977.

Levine, S.N. "Materials Inside the Body Struggle to Survive." *Materials Engineering,* July 1967.

Marks, G., and Beatty, W.K. *The Precious Metals of Medicine.* New York: Charles Scribner's Sons, 1975.

Miller, J.A. "Artificial Organs and Beyond." *Science News,* 3 September 1977.

Myers, G.H., and Parsonnet, V. "Engineering Inside the Body." *International Science and Technology,* February 1965.

Sonstegard, D.A., Mathews, L.S., and Kaufer, H. "The Surgical Replacement of the Human Knee Joint." *Scientific American,* January 1978.

Index

99

Picture Credits

Dr. William H. Dobelle: two pictures of artificial-vision system

Union Carbide: plutonium-powered pacemaker

Allied Pix Service: rechargeable pacemaker

Avco Corporation: four pictures of intra-aortic balloon pump

National Institutes of Health: three pictures of carotid sinus nerve stimulator

Michael Reese Medical Center: three pictures of total shoulder prosthesis

University of Michigan Health Sciences Information Service: artificial knee

RMI Company: titanium surgical implants

Battelle Columbus Laboratories: artificial muscle; two pictures of ceramic tooth root

University of Michigan Health Sciences Information Service: ear model; two pictures of ear prosthesis

Dr. Frank W. Clippinger (Duke University): prosthetic arm